THIS
DIARY
WILL CHANGE
YOUR
LIFE
2006

Extreme self-improvement!

D0308422

USER INSTRUCTIONS

Congratulations! You are the proud owner of This Diary Will Change Your Life 2006, the very latest in the cult bestselling series from authors Benrik Limited. Follow its instructions to the letter every week of the year, and your life will definitely change. Please note that Benrik's philosophy is one of life-change at any cost: it could be for the better, it might be for the worse. Only one thing is guaranteed: it will make the year 2006 impossible to forget, even with the help of expensive psychotherapy.

FEATURES

This symbol indicates that all readers are required to act together to realize the task's potential. From causing an international security alert to insulting alien civilizations, these are mass mobilization tasks that should shake society to its very foundations.

Orgasmic
Over the moon
Happy as Larry
Fine, thank you!
OK
So-so
Pissed off
Mad as hell
Deeply depressed
Suicidal

Mood chart™

It is crucial to monitor your mental state as you follow the Diary's prescriptions. Fill in the weekly mood charts by plotting your mood level every day of the week, and if your mood dips below the dotted line, seek immediate help. Compare your mood to the World Mood on www.thiswebsitewillchangeyourlife.com

NOTE TO OUR REGULAR USERS Thank you for your continuing loyalty to the Benrik brand. You make it what it is, and for that we are usually grateful. This year, you will note the following changes: we have moved to a weekly format, in order to make the Diary both more portable, and more affordable. In return, however, the new tasks are more substantial, and will require your sustained attention throughout the whole week. We have also given the actual diary sections their own pages. This is not an encouragement to fill them with anything other than our life-changing activities. We hope you enjoy 2006. May your life change yet again.

THIS DIARY WILL CHANGE YOUR LIFE BELONGS TO:

NAME Nico Franks

ADDRESS 32 Nelson Rd Ilkley West-Yorks

PHONE [HOME] 01943 430120

PHONE [WORK]

PHONE [MOBILE]

EMAIL nijfranks @ blueyonder .co.uk

COMPUTER IP ADDRESS

DATE OF BIRTH 07/06/90

SOCIAL SECURITY NUMBER 2AZ

ANNUAL SALARY £3150

TAX REF. NUMBER

DRIVING LICENCE NUMBER

BANK ACCOUNT NUMBER .... SORT CODE

MOTHER'S MAIDEN NAME/ONLINE PASSWORD Geddes

CREDIT CARD 1 .... EXPIRY .... PIN

CREDIT CARD 2 .... EXPIRY .... PIN

SAVINGS ACCOUNT NUMBER

BURGLAR ALARM CODE

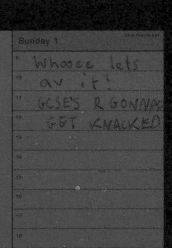

- - - - - - - - - - - - - - - - -

Blood Group in case of accident

CURRENT BLOOD GROUP

PREFERRED BLOOD GROUP

Should I become involved in an accident and require a transfusion, please use this opportunity to change my blood group as indicated above. Thank you.

MENTAL PREPARATION DAY

Before embarking on your new life, take a moment to reflect and find strength for the year ahead. Focus on how pathetic your life has been until now. How dysfunctional your family is. How miserable your friends are. How few of them still call you. How much you hate your boss. How much your boss hates you. How thin the ozone layer is becoming. How wholeheartedly you loathe everything about your current self. Once you have written off your old life, you are ready to turn the page. Good luck!

START YOUR OWN DIARY BLOG

Follow the Diary online starting today, with your very own blog on www.thiswebsitewillchangeyourlife.com! Join the many thousands of Benrik Bloggers and achieve instant fame. The most outrageous blogs rise to the top of the blog hit parade, where life is sweet, casual sex is a given, and publishing deals are done on a daily basis.

Sunday 1	NEW YEAR'S DAY
9	Whooee lets
10	av it!
11	GCSES R GONNA
12	GET KNACKED
13	
14	
15	
16	
17	
18	

YOUR VALUES ARE OUR TOILET PAPER

Benrik Limited was founded in 2003 by Ben Carey and Henrik Delehag. Benrik specialize in "extreme self-improvement", a promising new field which caters to those impatient with yoga, therapy, diets, and other tedious time-consuming discredited techniques. "Extreme self-improvement" requires permanent, radical and systematic life-change, to jolt us all out of the current coma of our collective imagination (post-9/11). This Diary Will Change Your Life in its various editions has sold over 250,000 copies worldwide so far, with no casualties reported amongst its users. Benrik Ltd also have interests in reality TV, branded content, graphic design and other society-enhancing activities. See www.benrik.co.uk for details.

Benrik Chair in Media Studies

Benrik Limited are pleased to announce they are endowing a Chair for university students who wish to study the Benrik oeuvre. The endowment may be claimed by any student who writes a substantial essay on Benrik's books, and receives a grade B or higher. The best essay, as judged by Benrik, will receive the endowment. The value of the endowment

BENRIK KEEPSAKE

Benrik are pleased to offer their readers this stunning unisex engraved locket, comprising an elegant gold-effect necklace, as well as solemn portraits of both Ben Carey and Henrik Delehag, founders of Benrik. Every true follower will want one, to help steel their resolve in the ways of life-change. It's available in a limited edition of 10,000, each at a very reasonable £99.99 + postage and packing. An indispensable bijou! Order now via the website.

Full-colour photographic portraits are included, and feature Henrik on the left and Ben on the right.

is £500. The Benrik Chair would probably suit the faculty of media studies best, although any humanities student may apply. Subjects include (but are not limited to): "Benrik's extreme self-help philosophy and its contribution to the cultural landscape"; "the Diary Will Change Your Life series and what its success reveals about the human condition at the dawn of the third millennium"; "Wittgenstein after Benrik". Potential recipients must apply via contact@benrik.co.uk for subject approval. Deadline for entries (completed and graded essays): 30 June 2006. Benrik's decisions are final. No correspondence will be entered into. The successful essay will be published on www.thiswebsitewillchangeyourlife.com. To your pens!

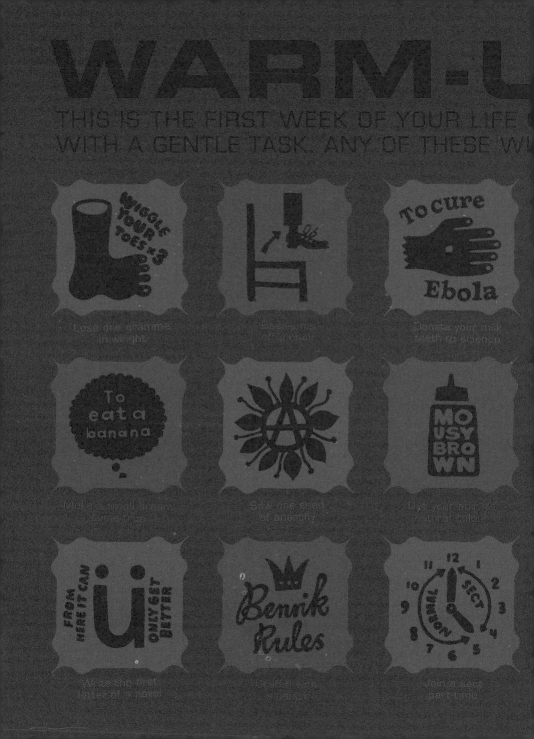

Monday 2 BANK HOLIDAY UK AND IRELAND	Tuesday 3 BANK HOLIDAY SCOTLAND	Wednesday 4
9		
10		
11		
12		
13		
14		
15		
16		
17		
18		

Thursday 5

| 9 |
| 10 |
| 11 |
| 12 |
| 13 |
| 14 |
| 15 |
| 16 |
| 17 |
| 18 |

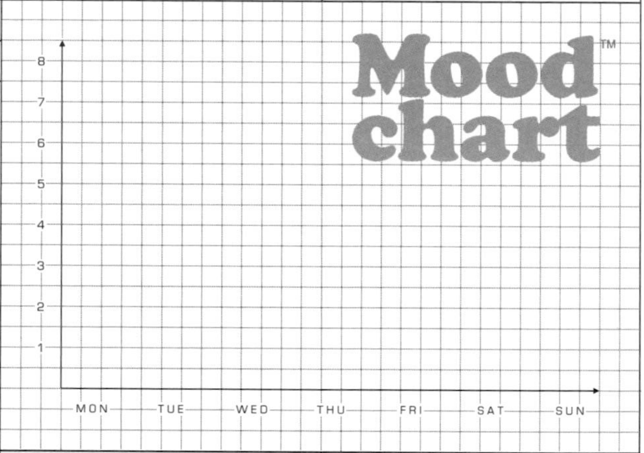

Mood chart™

8 7 6 5 4 3 2 1

MON TUE WED THU FRI SAT SUN

Friday 6	Saturday 7	Sunday 8
9		
10		
11		
12		
13		
14		
15		
16		
17		
18		

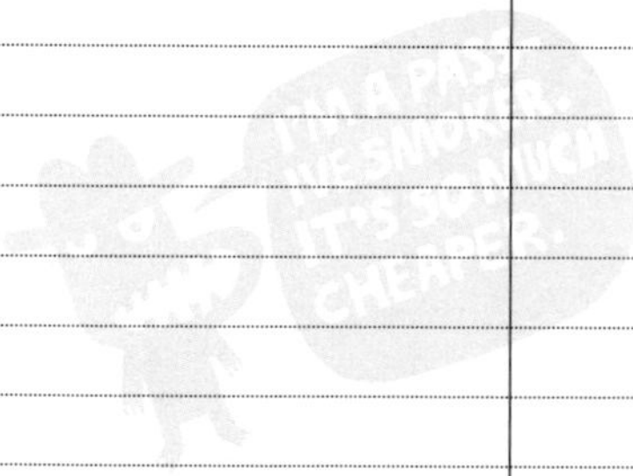

Monday 9	Tuesday 10	Wednesday 11
9		
10		
11		
12		
13		
14		
15		
16		
17		
18		

Thursday 12	Friday 13	Saturday 14
9		
10		
11		
12		
13		
14		
15		
16		
17		
18		

Sunday 15	
9	
10	
11	
12	
13	
14	
15	
16	
17	
18	

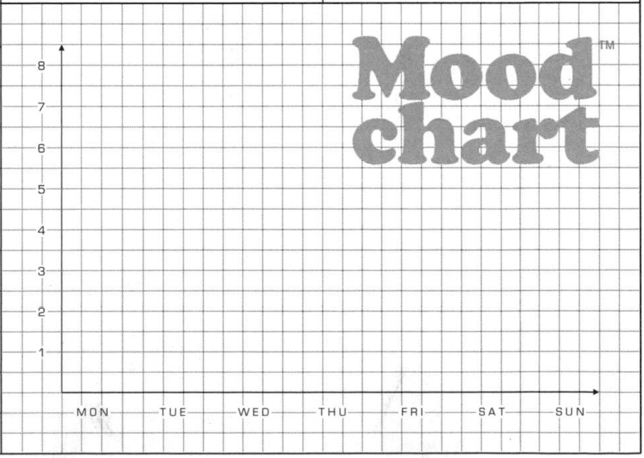

Mood chart™

8
7
6
5
4
3
2
1

MON — TUE — WED — THU — FRI — SAT — SUN

Be a pathological liar

I never got your e-mail.

I paid you for that coffee a minute ago.

This porno mag was in your drawer.

The president just got shot!

B patho liar we

I gave you that report yesterday!

You don't have a daddy.

No, I'm not married.

Trust me. I'm a doctor.

This week lie yo absolutely every much more stim

They
give me
one week
to live.

Of course
I'm wearing
a condom.

I double-
checked your
parachute
myself.

a

ogical

or a

ek

He fancies
you like
crazy, he
told me so.

Don't
worry
it's not
hot.

What do you
mean you're my
wife? I've never
even met you
before.

He's a
well-known
child molester,
I read it in
the paper.

r ass off about

ing and enjoy a

ating existence.

MINI-PROSTITUTION WEEK SELL A VERY MINOR SEXUAL FAVOUR

It's the oldest job in the world, yet most people never even consider it. There's no reason why you have to jump in at the deep end with full-blown sex with strangers. Find out if prostitution is for you by starting small: offer someone a kiss on the cheek for £1 perhaps; caress a neighbour's hand for £3; let the checkout girl squeeze your bottom for £10. Who knows, you may discover your true vocation.

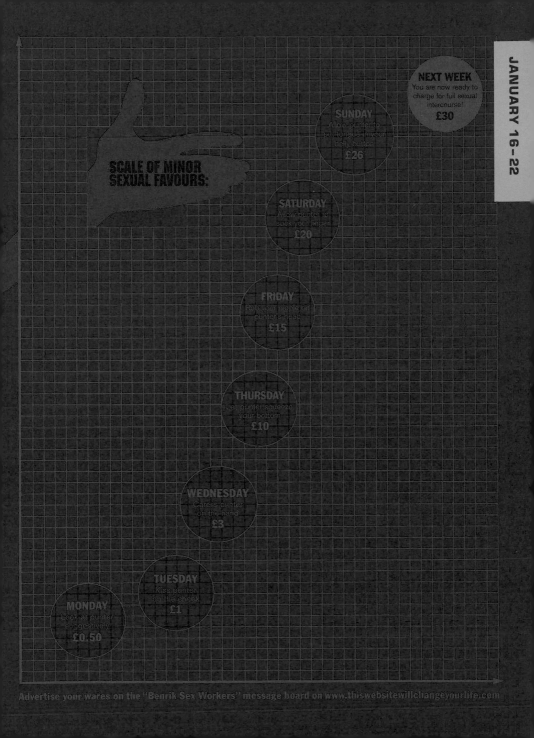

SCALE OF MINOR
SEXUAL FAVOURS:

NEXT WEEK
You are now ready to
charge for full sexual
intercourse!
£30

SUNDAY
Allow punter to
put tongue in your
belly button
£26

SATURDAY
Allow punter to
suck your finger
£20

FRIDAY
Rub your nipple on
punter's head
£15

THURSDAY
Let punter squeeze
your bottom
£10

WEDNESDAY
Caress punter
on the hand
£3

TUESDAY
Kiss punter
on the cheek
£1

MONDAY
Look at punter
suggestively
£0.50

Mini-prostitution Week

Monday 16	Tuesday 17	Wednesday 18
9		
10		
11		
12		
13		
14		
15		
16		
17		
18		

Thursday 19

| 9 |
| 10 |
| 11 |
| 12 |
| 13 |
| 14 |
| 15 |
| 16 |
| 17 |
| 18 |

Mood chart™

8
7
6
5
4
3
2
1

MON — TUE — WED — THU — FRI — SAT — SUN

Friday 20	Saturday 21	Sunday 22
9		
10		
11		
12		
13		
14		
15		
16		
17		
18		

I CAN'T TELL YOU ANYTHING ABOUT MY JOB, BUT JUST THE SAME I'M A VERY IMPORTANT PERSON AND DESERVE A LOT OF RESPECT.

Prepare for Chinese World Domination

Monday 23	Tuesday 24	Wednesday 25
9		
10		
11		
12		
13		
14		
15		
16		
17		
18		

Thursday 26	Friday 27	Saturday 28
9		
10		
11		
12		
13		
14		
15		
16		
17		
18		

Sunday 29   CHINESE NEW YEAR

9
10
11
12
13
14
15
16
17
18

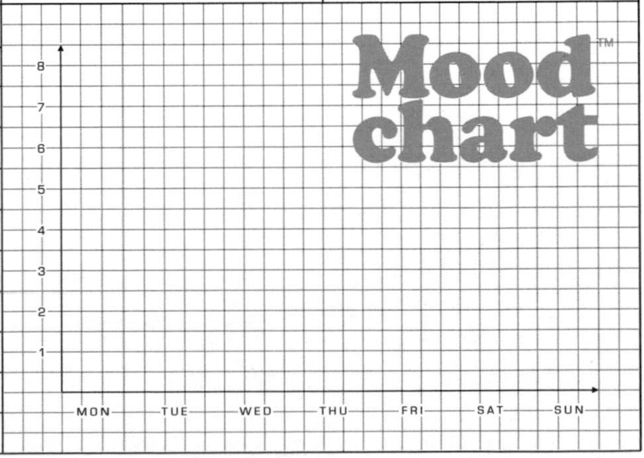

Mood chart™

8
7
6
5
4
3
2
1

MON — TUE — WED — THU — FRI — SAT — SUN

This week, prepare for Chinese World Domination

The 21st century will witness China's inexorable rise to global prominence. With a population of over 1.3 billion and an economy growing at nearly 10% a year, China is on an inevitable geopolitical collision course with the West. The West may win this contest, but don't bank on it; this week, make sure you acquire the skills needed to survive under Chinese occupation. Mandarin will be compulsory of course – get a head start here.

MANDARIN

A	阿	N	恩
B	波	O	喔
C	雌	P	泼
D	得	Q	欺
E	鹅	R	日
F	佛	S	思
G	哥	T	特
H	喝	U	乌
I	衣	V	微
J	基	W	屋
K	科	X	希
L	勒	Y	也
M	摸	Z	资

Dealing with the occupying power will be much easier if you understand their world view. Confucius (551–479 BC) is the best place to start. Meditate his wise words, and you will avoid many a dangerous faux pas.

CONFUCIAN ANALECTS

BOOK I.

Chapter I. 1. The Master said, "Is it not pleasant to learn with a constant perseverance and application?
2. "Is it not delightful to have friends coming from distant quarters?
3. "Is he not a man of complete virtue, who feels no discomposure though men may take no note of him?"

Chapter II. 1. The philosopher Yu said, "They are few who, being filial and fraternal, are fond of offending against their superiors. There have been none, who, not liking to offend against their superiors, have been fond of stirring up confusion.
2. "The superior man bends his attention to what is radical. That being established, all practical courses naturally grow up. Filial piety and fraternal submission! Are they not the root of all benevolent actions?"

Chapter III. The Master said, "Fine words and an insinuating appearance are seldom associated with true virtue."

Chapter IV. The philosopher Tsang said, "I daily examine myself on three points: whether, in transacting business for others, I may have been not faithful; whether, in intercourse with friends, I may have been not sincere; whether I may have not mastered and practised the instructions of my teacher?"

Chapter V. The Master said, "To rule a country of a thousand chariots, there must be reverent attention to business, and sincerity; economy in expenditure, and love for men; and the employment of the people at the proper seasons."

Chapter VI. The Master said, "A youth, when at home, should be filial, and, abroad, respectful to his elders. He should

be earnest and truthful. He should overflow in love to all, and cultivate the friendship of the good. When he has time and opportunity, after the performance of these things, he should employ them in polite studies."

Chapter VII. Tsze-hsia said, "If a man withdraws his mind from the love of beauty, and applies it as sincerely to the love of the virtuous; if, in serving his parents, he can exert his utmost strength; if, in serving his prince, he can devote his life; if, in his intercourse with his friends, his words are sincere: although men say that he has not learned, I will certainly say that he has."

Chapter VIII. 1. The Master said, "If the scholar be not grave, he will not call forth any veneration, and his learning will not be solid.
2. "Hold faithfulness and sincerity as first principles.
3. "Have no friends not equal to yourself.
4. "When you have faults, do not fear to abandon them."

Chapter IX. The philosopher Tsang said, "Let there be a careful attention to perform the funeral rites to parents, and let them be followed when long gone with the ceremonies of sacrifice; then the virtue of the people will resume its proper excellence."

Chapter X. 1. Tsze-ch'in asked Tsze-kung, saying, "When our master comes to any country, he does not fail to learn all about its government. Does he ask his information? Or is it given to him?"
2. Tsze-kung said, "Our master is benign, upright, courteous, temperate, and complaisant, and thus he gets his information. The master's mode of asking information! Is it not different from that of other men?"

Chapter XI. The Master said, "While a man's father is alive, look at the bent of his will; when his father is dead, look at his conduct. If for three years he does not alter from the way of his father, he may be called filial."

Chapter XII. The philosopher Yu said, "In practising the rules of propriety, a natural ease is to be prized. In the ways prescribed by the kings, this is the excellent quality,"

THIS WEEK, CAUSE AN INTERNATIONA

CONSPIRACY THEORISTS HAVE PO

A SUPERSECRET TRANSNATIONA

ALL ELECTRONIC COMMUNICATIO

SYSTEM ALLEGEDLY "RED FLAGS"

TO INTERCEPT TERRORIST OR OT

TEST THIS THEORY THROUGHOUT

MANY OF THE FOLLOWING KEY

EMAILS. YOU WILL KNOW THE

ARRESTED AND QUESTIONED

KEYWORDS INCLUDE: ATF OSAM

NASA KASHMIR TIMER TWIN

BESLAN OKLAHOMA CITY GUA

CIA RIFLE NSA HANDGUN SEM

RUMSFELD ASSAULT GUN TER

KORESH ZARQAWI SHARON MO

SADDAM HUSSEIN HIS GEORG

CELL APOCALYPSE SCOTLAN

SECURITY MELTDOWN. FOR YEARS
TED THE EXISTENCE OF ECHELO
EFFORT BY THE WEST TO SPY O
S, FROM PHONES TO EMAILS. TH
RTAIN KEYWORDS IN AN ATTEMP
ERWISE SUBVERSIVE MESSAGES.
HE WEEK BY INCORPORATING AS
ORDS AS POSSIBLE INTO YOUR
HEORY IS CORRECT IF YOU ARE
AT GREAT LENGTH. GOODBYE.
BIN LADEN FBI WACO MILITIA
OWERS RUBY RIDGE PENTAGON
ANAMO WORLD TRADE CENTRE
X AL QAEDA HOSTAGE MARTY
OR SM BOMB DRUG A   /11
SAD FALLUJA M16 REV
W. BUSH TERRORIST
ARD CID CHECHNYA

Monday 30	Tuesday 31	Wednesday 1
9		
10		
11		
12		
13		
14		
15		
16		
17		
18		

Thursday 2

9	
10	
11	
12	
13	
14	
15	
16	
17	
18	

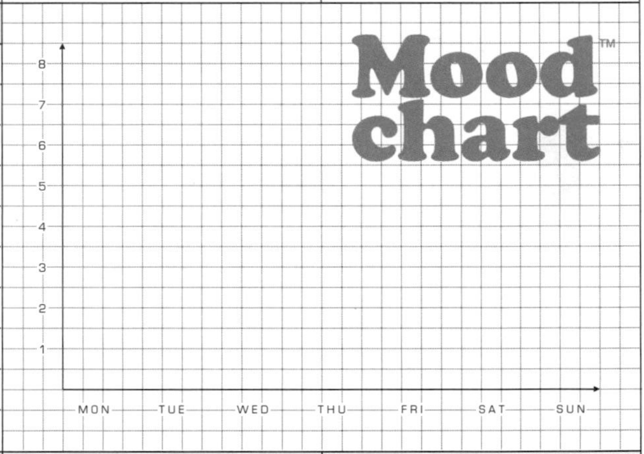

Mood chart™

8
7
6
5
4
3
2
1

MON — TUE — WED — THU — FRI — SAT — SUN

Friday 3	Saturday 4	Sunday 5
9		
10		
11		
12		
13		
14		
15		
16		
17		
18		

Monday 6

9

10

11

12

13

14

15

16

17

18

Thursday 9

9

10

11

12

13

14

15

16

17

18

Friday 10

Saturday 11

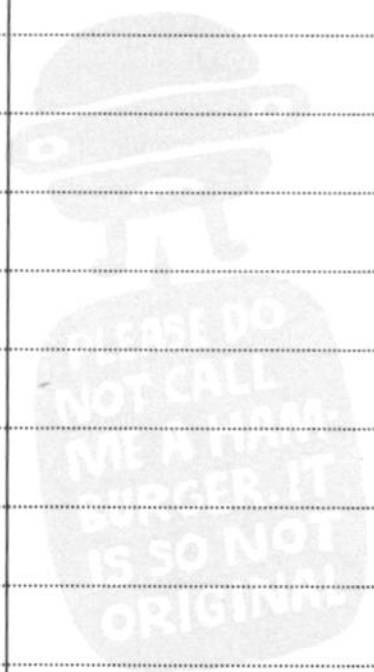

Sunday 12

9

10

11

12

13

14

15

16

17

18

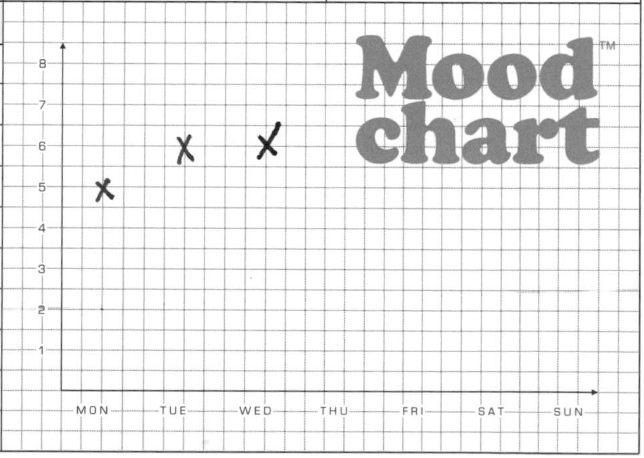

Mood chart™

MON	TUE	WED	THU	FRI	SAT	SUN

8
7
6
5
4
3
2
1

...ces the
e from the
e instant

Here are some
concrete events
that you may
confidently predict.

Arriving from the future: you must follow correct procedure.

1) You must arrive at night, preferably during a storm, near power lines. Any evidence of electromagnetic disturbance will enhance your credibility. 2) You must arrive naked. Clothes do not travel well through time. Also, "Made in China" labels will detract from your story. 3) You must claim urgent police protection against the androids who have been sent to kill you. If anyone questions their existence, claim that *they* are the fucking android and try to get them shot in the ensuing panic. 4) You must pick a credible year. 2007 is too close to be of interest. 56802 is not believable, unless you sport antennae. 2049 has a nice ring to it. 5) If you are single, why not try the chat-up line, "I've been sent from the future to save you." It's guaranteed foolproof. 6) During any temporary stay in psychiatric institutions, avoid harping on about imminent nuclear holocausts; it unsettles doctors and patients alike. 7) Once you've achieved your fame and fortune, knock yourself out, claim amnesia, and return to normal present-based life.

The key to this of course is correctly prophesying future events.

Thanks to Benrik and their followers, this is now entirely possible.

At some point in 2006, Kajagoogoo's "Too Shy" will reach the Top 10 again.

On Sunday 20 August, dogpoo will dominate the media.

On Friday 30 June 2006, a French tourist will sue the British Museum.

The week of September 4 will see a rash of strange and unexplained murders.

By Sunday 15 October, aliens will invade the Earth, causing some serious damage.

ATTRACT YOUR

The fundamental law of relationships is that "opposites attract". On the occasion of Valentine's Day, improve

OPPOSITE

your love life dramatically by trying to seduce the person most unlike you.

FINDING YOUR OPPOSITE

Tick as many of these boxes as possible. If your potential match offers at least 10 contrasting features, you'll know you've found the opposite of your life... If you are already in a relationship, and you tick fewer than 10 of these, then ditch your partner, for they are virtually your clone.

		Tick!
If you are tall	They must be short	☐
If you are young	They must be old	☐
If you are thin	They must be fat	☐
If you are bright	They must be dumb	☐
If you are a beauty	They must be a beast	☐
If you like meat	They must be vegan	☐
If you like chess	They must like wrestling	☐
If you like a cuddle	They must like a whipping	☐
If you like animals	They must like fur	☐
If you like laughing	They must like crying	☐
If you enjoy travelling	They must enjoy sitting	☐
If you enjoy the arts	They must enjoy darts	☐
If you enjoy singing	They must enjoy shouting	☐
If you enjoy smoking	They must suffer from lung cancer	☐
If you enjoy peace and quiet	They must suffer from Tourette's	☐
If you vote left	They must vote far-right	☐
If you play sports	They must play with themselves	☐
If you believe in God	They must believe in aliens	☐
If you want kids	They must want the snip	☐
If you love life	They must love Lucifer	☐

And so on...

Monday 13	Tuesday 14 VALENTINE'S DAY	Wednesday 15
9		
10		
11		
12		
13		
14		
15		
16		
17		
18		

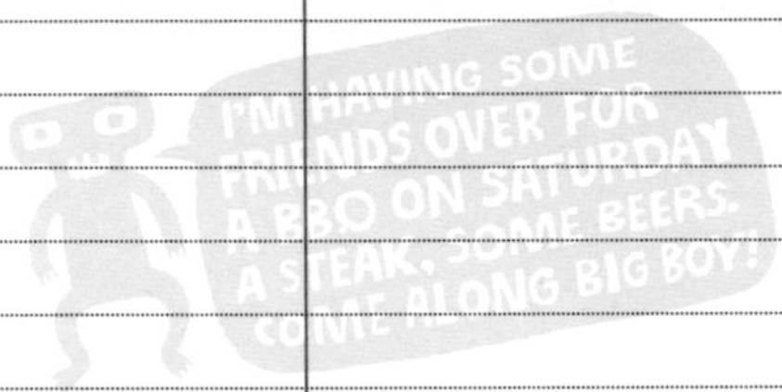

Thursday 16

9	
10	
11	
12	
13	
14	
15	
16	
17	
18	

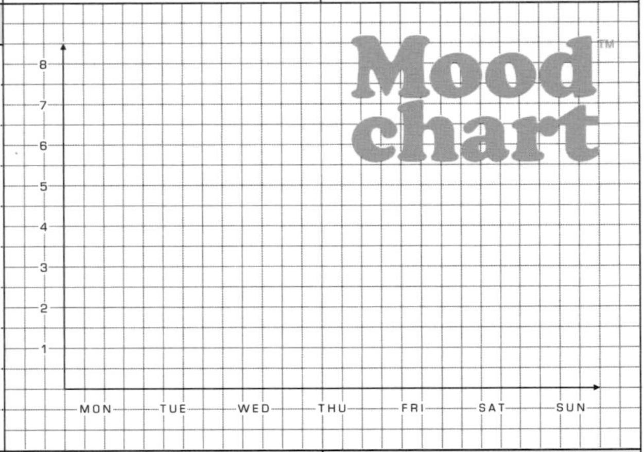

Mood chart™

8
7
6
5
4
3
2
1

MON — TUE — WED — THU — FRI — SAT — SUN

Friday 17	Saturday 18	Sunday 19
9		
10		
11		
12		
13		
14		
15		
16		
17		
18		

Monday 20	Tuesday 21	Wednesday 22
9		
10		
11		
12		
13		
14		
15		
16		
17		
18		

Thursday 23	Friday 24	Saturday 25
9		
10		
11		
12		
13		
14		
15		
16		
17		
18		

Sunday 26
9
10
11
12
13
14
15
16
17
18

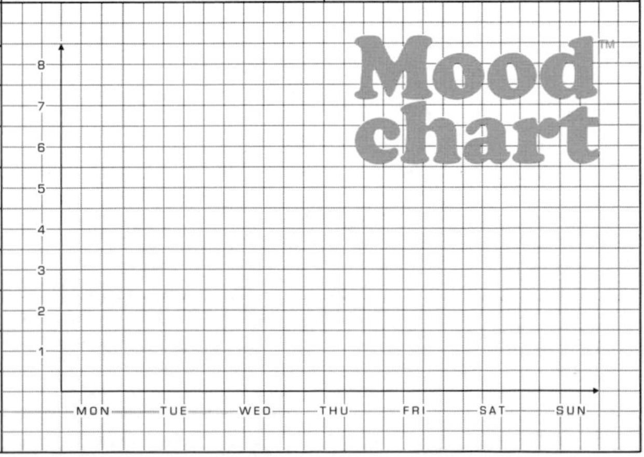

Mood chart™

8
7
6
5
4
3
2
1

MON — TUE — WED — THU — FRI — SAT — SUN

Slavery Week

VOLUNTEER TO BECOME SOMEONE'S SLAVE FOR SEVEN DAYS

Slavery is the new yoga. What better way to stop worrying about all life's responsibilities than to hand them over to someone else? Register your details on www.thiswebsitewillchangeyourlife.com today Monday, and by tonight you will have a proud new owner for the week.

BIRD! CATCH IT!

NOW TAKE ME TO THE MUSEUM!

I NEED TO PRACTICE SOME PARALYSING KARATE TECHNIQUES ON YOU NOW I'M AFRAID!

BE MY HUMAN CLOCK TODAY PLEASE

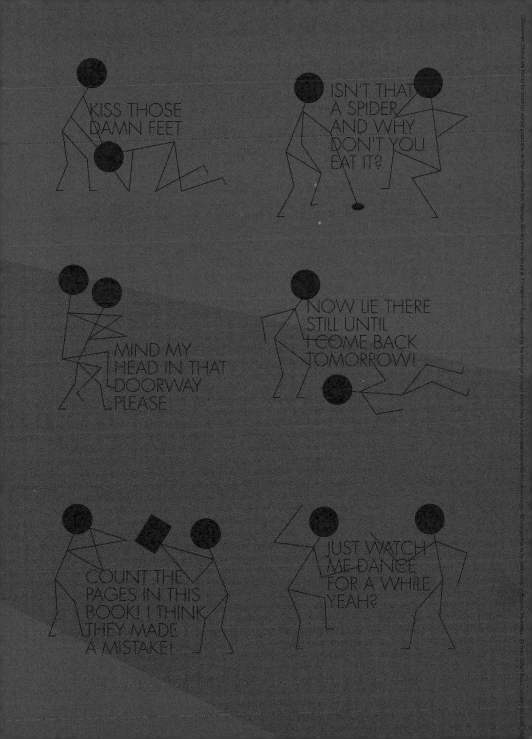

Commit all Seven Sins this week

Monday
LUST
Ogle a particularly attractive member of the opposite sex.

Tuesday
ENVY

Discover who their partner is and let jealousy enwrap you.

Wednesday
GREED

Even if you're already loved up, decide you could do with something on the side.

and earn yourself a place in hell

Thursday
ANGER
Rage, when the object of your desire politely tells you to stop ogling them.

Friday
SLOTH
Let despondency get the better of you and spend the day in bed – alone.

Saturday
GLUTTONY
To forget the pain of rejection, what better than an alcohol and chocolate orgy?

Sunday
PRIDE

You never fancied them anyway, they're simply not in your league.

Commit all Seven Sins

Monday 27	Tuesday 28	Wednesday 1
9		
10		
11		
12		
13		
14		
15		
16		
17		
18		

Thursday 2	
9	
10	
11	
12	
13	
14	
15	
16	
17	
18	

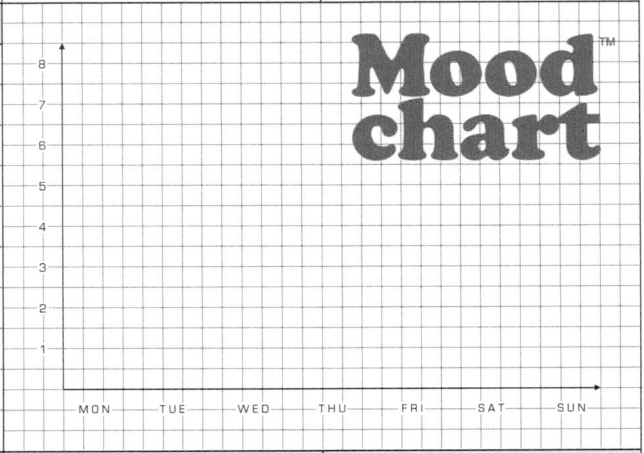

Mood chart™

8
7
6
5
4
3
2
1

MON — TUE — WED — THU — FRI — SAT — SUN

Friday 3	Saturday 4	Sunday 5
9		
10		
11		
12		
13		
14		
15		
16		
17		
18		

Monday 6	Tuesday 7	Wednesday 8
9		
10		
11		
12		
13		
14		
15		
16		
17		
18		

Thursday 9	Friday 10	Saturday 11
9		
10		
11		
12		
13		
14		
15		
16		
17		
18		

Sunday 12
9
10
11
12
13
14
15
16
17
18

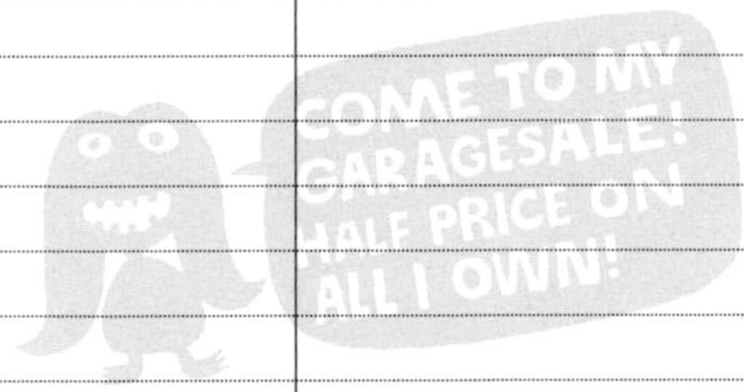

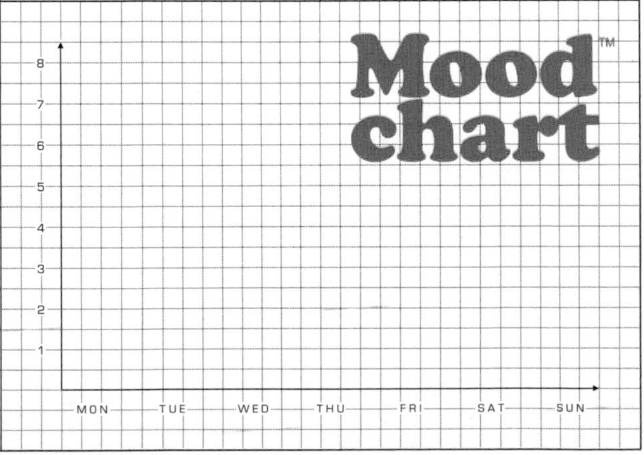

COME TO MY GARAGE SALE! HALF PRICE ON ALL I OWN!

Mood chart™

8 7 6 5 4 3 2 1

MON TUE WED THU FRI SAT SUN

KAJAGOO TOO

THIS WEEK, HELP FIX THE CHARTS

Everyone knows the charts are fixed by record companies. Don't let them impose their feeble marketing plans on the nation. If every single Diary reader buys the same surprise single this week, we will sabotage the music industry's machinations and lay bare its hypocrisy. Rock on!

Where are they now? After their *White Feathers* album, which featured the international No. 1 "Too Shy", Kajagoogoo parted company with their flamboyant lead singer Limahl, who allegedly felt that his songwriting contribution was not sufficiently recognized. Kajagoogoo released two more albums, but neither enjoyed great commercial success and the band split up. After leaving the band, Limahl (aka Chris Hamill) started a solo career, scoring a hit with the title song for the film *The Neverending Story*. Since then he has met with mixed success as a producer, though TV's recent appetite for comeback celebrities has raised his profile again. Breaking news: Nick, Stuart and Steve are re-forming Kajagoogoo! Watch this space!

WRITE TO KAJAGOOGOO VIA:
INFORMATION@NICKBEGGS.CO.UK
WRITE TO LIMAHL VIA:
KONTAKT@LIMAHL-OFFICIAL-FAN-CLUB.DE
WON'T THEY BE SURPRISED!

Guitarist Steve Askew runs his own recording studio.

GOO
SHY

Keyboards man Stuart
Neale is a business
developement manager.

Frontman
Limahl is still
looking good!

Ex-drummer Jez
Strode rents
music gear.

Bassist Nick Beggs
writes for Bass
Guitar Magazine.

Mouth obscenities to passing strangers

Monday 13	Tuesday 14	Wednesday 15
9		
10		
11		
12		
13		
14		
15		
16		
17		
18		

Thursday 16

9	
10	
11	
12	
13	
14	
15	
16	
17	
18	

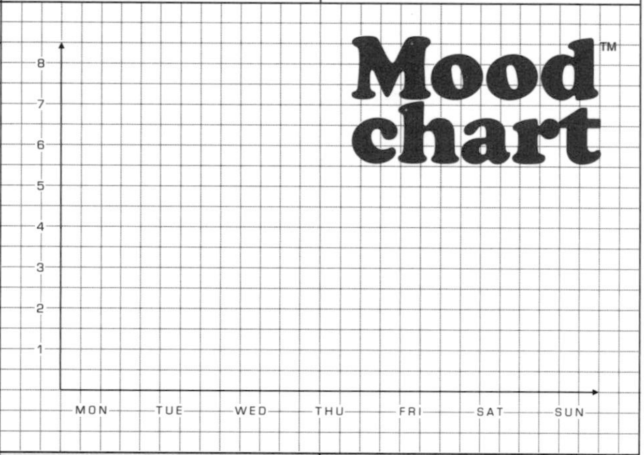

Mood chart™

8
7
6
5
4
3
2
1

MON — TUE — WED — THU — FRI — SAT — SUN

Friday 17 ST. PATRICK'S DAY	Saturday 18	Sunday 19
9		
10		
11		
12		
13		
14		
15		
16		
17		
18		

Monday 20	Tuesday 21	Wednesday 22
9		
10		
11		
12		
13		
14		
15		
16		
17		
18		

Thursday 23	Friday 24	Saturday 25
9		
10		
11		
12		
13		
14		
15		
16		
17		
18		

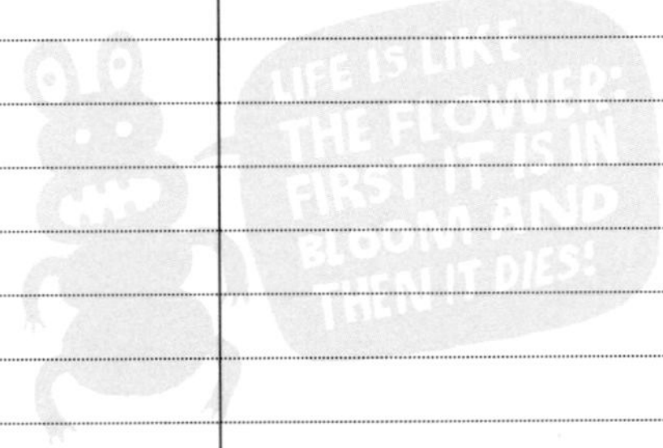

LIFE IS LIKE THE FLOWER: FIRST IT IS IN BLOOM THEN IT DIES!

Sunday 26	
9	
10	
11	
12	
13	
14	
15	
16	
17	
18	

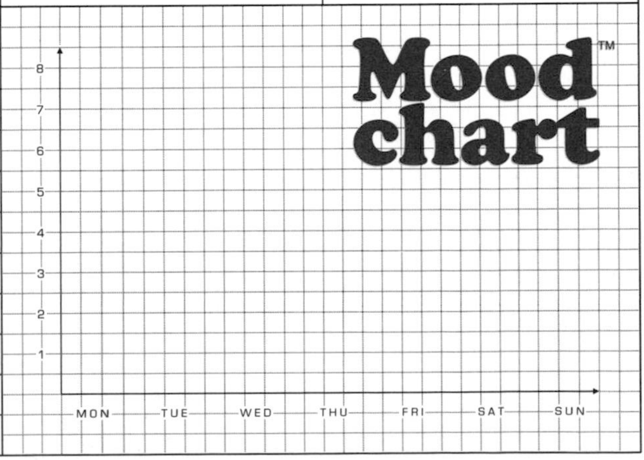

Mood chart™

MON TUE WED THU FRI SAT SUN

This week, pretend you're a doctor

CASE 1

Pedestrian knocked over by car

CASE 2

Woman starts contractions on public transport

WRITE YOUR NAME HERE IN BLOCK LETTERS

FOR PRESIDENT IN 2008!!!

Yes! I support..
FOR PRESIDENT IN 2008!
Name:...
....
Address:...
....
Signature:...

I contribute the sum of
$2,000 ☐ **$1,000** ☐ **$500** ☐ **Other** ☐

Enlarge and photocopy x1000

THIS WEEK, RUN FOR U.S. PRESIDENT

The next US presidential election isn't due until 4 November 2008, but to stand a serious chance, you must start to run now! Winning is the culmination of years of preparation, grassroots campaigning, political networking, and last but not least, fundraising. You will need ten million dollars minimum if you wish to be taken seriously. Start today, by gathering cash and signatures to support your bid. Good luck!

Following their successful www.globalvote2004.org campaign, Benrik are pushing through a 28th amendment to the US Constitution that would allow foreigners to stand. Our case is based on the democratic principle that people should have a say in who determines their destiny. As the world's sole superpower, the US now has a huge impact beyond its borders, effectively ruling the planet. Democracy therefore demands that the rest of the world should be able to put forward candidates. The Benrik amendment has been received by the Senate and is making its way through the lengthy administrative procedure required for ratification. It should be in place by 2008 though, so get busy.

IMPORTANT! FILING YOUR CANDIDACY: Once you receive contributions or make expenditures in excess of $5,000, you must register with the Federal Election Commission (FEC). Within 15 days of reaching that $5,000 threshold, you must file a Statement of Candidacy authorizing a principal campaign committee to raise and spend funds on your behalf. Within 10 days of that filing, your principal campaign committee must submit a Statement of Organization. Your campaign will thereafter report its receipts and disbursements on a regular basis. Federal Election Commission, FPC Desk (Foreign Presidential Candidates), 999 E Street, NW, Washington, DC 20463, USA

Run for US president

Monday 27	Tuesday 28	Wednesday 29
9		
10		
11		
12		
13		
14		
15		
16		
17		
18		

Thursday 30		
9		
10		
11		
12		
13		
14		
15		
16		
17		
18		

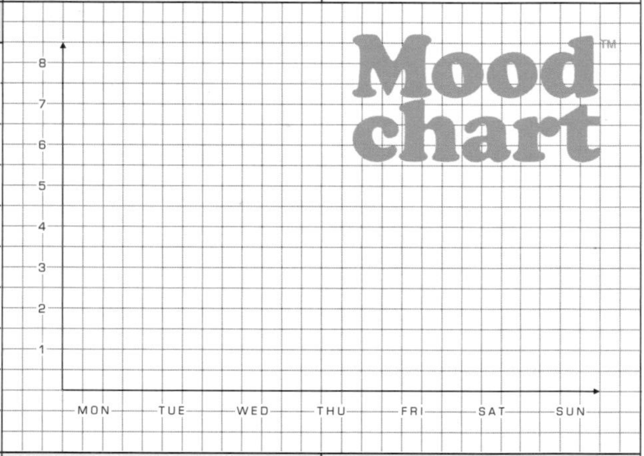

Mood chart ™

8
7
6
5
4
3
2
1

MON — TUE — WED — THU — FRI — SAT — SUN

Friday 31	Saturday 1	Sunday 2
9		
10		
11		
12		
13		
14		
15		
16		
17		
18		

Monday 3	Tuesday 4	Wednesday 5
9		
10		
11		
12		
13		
14		
15		
16		
17		
18		

Thursday 6	Friday 7	Saturday 8
9		
10		
11		
12		
13		
14		
15		
16		
17		
18		

Sunday 9

| 9 |
| 10 |
| 11 |
| 12 |
| 13 |
| 14 |
| 15 |
| 16 |
| 17 |
| 18 |

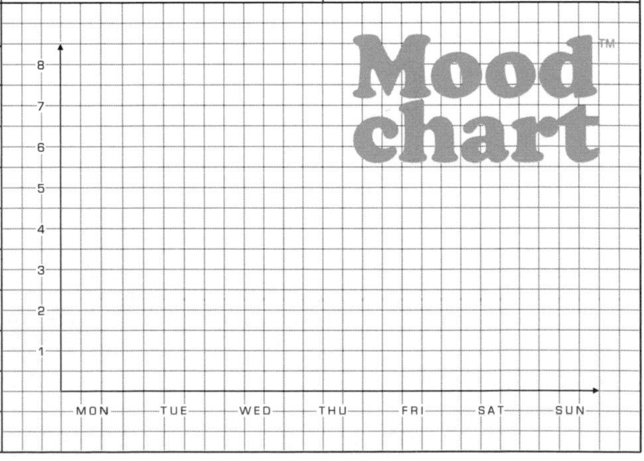

I LIKE SALT
AND PEPPER ON
THE DISMEMBE-
RED BODIES TOO
FOR DINNER

Mood™
chart

8
7
6
5
4
3
2
1

MON — TUE — WED — THU — FRI — SAT — SUN

Step on as many people's feet as possible

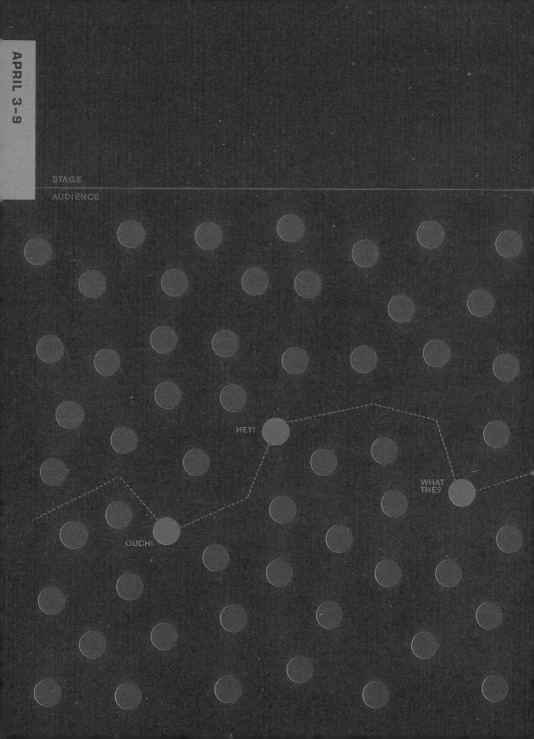

This week, step on as many people's feet as possible, claiming it was an accident.

AAARGH!

MEEOWWW!

POFF!

This week, ask billionaires for money

Billionaires are happy to give money to worthy causes, like AIDS or malaria. Why shouldn't they give some to you? Write to the world's richest this week asking if they could spare you just 0.01% of their fortune. It's unlikely you'll get replies from all of them, but you never know. If you don't ask, you don't get.

BILL GATES Age: 50
Marital status: Married with 3 children
Estimated worth: $48 billion
Source of billions: Microsoft empire
Estimated generosity to complete strangers: 6/10
Address: c/o Microsoft, Redmond, WA 98052, USA

WARREN BUFFETT Age: 75
Marital status: Widowed, 3 children
Estimated worth: $44 billion
Source of billions: Investments
Estimated generosity to complete strangers: 6/10
Address: c/o Berkshire Hathaway, 1440 Kiewit Plaza, Omaha, NE 68131, USA

Dear Mr Gates,

I'm a huge huge fan of all your software products, particularly the Windows range. I use them all the time and I can honestly say they've made my working life a whole lot easier. So thanks a bunch! By the way, I read that you're into good causes and the like; could you see your way to sparing me a few millions (nothing to a man such as you)? I would spend a lot of it on Microsoft stuff, so that way you can't lose. Let me know and keep up the good work!

Yours gratefully

Sample Letter

Dear Mr Buffett,

I have a fantastic idea for an investment for you: me. I read that you go for long-term prospects. Well, that's me all over! With just a few piddly millions from you, I can go a long way, you'll see. Some of my ideas include: robot bed-maker, maps of the Internet (colour), a totally new type of spaceship. I would be prepared to let you in on the action (let's say 10%). Think it through, and call me sometime. Nebraska is a bit far for me to travel, but we could meet in Boston perhaps, I'm going there later in the year to visit my uncle.

Kind regards

Sample Letter

LAKSHMI MITTAL Age: 55
Marital status: Married with 2 children
Estimated worth: $27 billion
Source of billions: Steel
Estimated generosity to complete strangers: 5/10
Address: 18/19 Kensington Palace Gardens,
London W84JJD, UK

Dear Mr Mittal,

Who would have thought there was so much
money to be made in steel! Well, I guess there
is, and that you've got most of it, well done.
Now, I myself am a businessman of sorts, and I
have a business proposition for you. In exchange
for a very small proportion of your fortune
(0.01% max) I would devote my waking hours
to spreading the word about your generosity.
Billionaires get a bad rap for being greedy
exploitative fat cats. Only the other day in the
pub, someone was slagging you off (I won't
repeat the language), and so I smacked him
for you, for free. Believe me, you need my help!
Call me soon.

P.S. I can get you the guy's hospital room number
if you want to take things further.

PRINCE ALWALEED BIN TALAL ALSAUD Age: 48
Marital status: Married with 2 children
Estimated worth: $25 billion
Source of billions: nephew of the Saudi king
Estimated generosity to complete strangers: 8/10
Address: c/o Kingdom Holding Company, P.O.
Box 2, Riyadh, 11321, Saudi Arabia

Dear Excellency,

Your reputation as a kindly and giving prince,
second to none, has reached my ears.
Indeed, of all the Saudi princes, you are by far
my favourite. I come to you with a modest plea.
Your land is blessed with the black gold oil,
which you have wisely used to invest in a wide
variety of multinational corporations. My own
land is barren, and so I was wondering if you
could spare a few gallons. Or you could just
transfer the cash ($2,500,000 should do the
trick). Thank you and may your family prosper
and your business be favoured by the gods.

CARLOS SLIM HELU Age: 66
Marital status: Widowed, 6 children
Estimated worth: $29 billion
Source of billions: Telecoms
Estimated generosity to complete strangers: 9/10
Address: c/o Grupo Carso, Miguel de Cervantes
Saavedra 255, 11520 Mexico City, Mexico

Hola Carlos!

I went to Mexico once in 1995 on a tour
and I enjoyed your fine country immensely.
Friendly people, great tequila, hot ladies,
caramba as you like to say. I am now back in
England where I live, and was wondering if I
could bother you for a few pesos! The generosity
of your people is legendary, and I'm sure you
live up to it. I have modest needs: a couple of
million dollars would be plenty. That's about 22
million pesos — enough to keep the margaritas
flowing! Seriously though, I need it. Gracias
amigo and hasta la vista!

INGVAR KAMPRAD Age: 79
Marital status: Married with 4 children
Estimated worth: $22 billion
Source of billions: Ikea
Estimated generosity to complete strangers: 6/10
Address: 1066 Epalinges, Lausanne, Switzerland

Hallo Ingvar!

I am Swedish like you, and I have been
shopping at Ikea and eating your meatballs ever
since I was born. I used to love those meatballs!
Though now I am a vegetarian. The furniture is
still good though, especially because it is cheap.
You see, living in Sweden, not like you in
Switzerland, I have to pay 90% tax, and so
despite my efforts, I am one of the poor. If you
could give me 0.01% of your money, that would
make me happy. It is probably less than I spent
in your stores! Don't worry, I will not tell
anyone else in Sweden. Thanx a bunch!

Ask a billionaire for money

Monday 10
9
10
11
12
13
14
15
16
17
18

Tuesday 11
9
10
11
12
13
14
15
16
17
18

Wednesday 12
9
10
11
12
13
14
15
16
17
18

Thursday 13
9
10
11
12
13
14
15
16
17
18

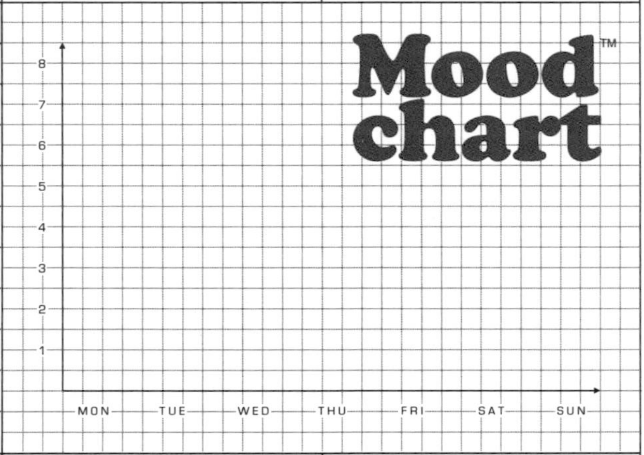

Mood chart ™

8
7
6
5
4
3
2
1

MON — TUE — WED — THU — FRI — SAT — SUN

Friday 14   GOOD FRIDAY
9
10
11
12
13
14
15
16
17
18

Saturday 15
9
10
11
12
13
14
15
16
17
18

Sunday 16   EASTER SUNDAY
9
10
11
12
13
14
15
16
17
18

Imaginary Friend Week

Monday 17 EASTER MONDAY	Tuesday 18	Wednesday 19
9		
10		
11		
12		
13		
14		
15		
16		
17		
18		

Thursday 20	Friday 21	Saturday 22
9		
10		
11		
12		
13		
14		
15		
16		
17		
18		

Sunday 23

| 9 |
| 10 |
| 11 |
| 12 |
| 13 |
| 14 |
| 15 |
| 16 |
| 17 |
| 18 |

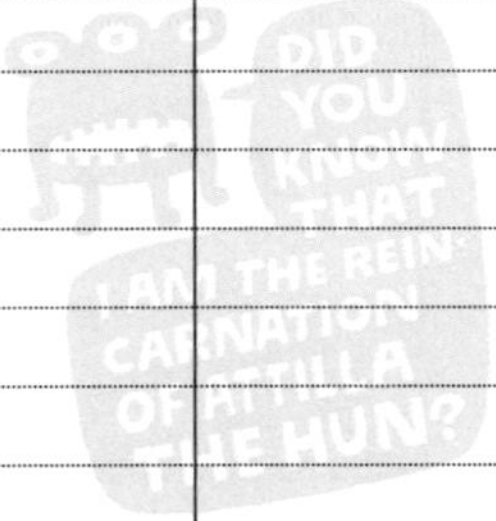

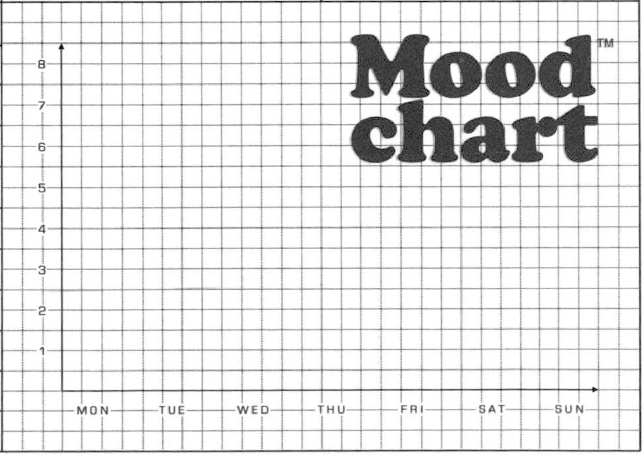

Mood chart ™

8
7
6
5
4
3
2
1

MON — TUE — WED — THU — FRI — SAT — SUN

IMAGINAR

Studies indicate that the more l
likely to be. So take the lead an

Monday: Give him a name.

Pick something sensible like George or Sarah. "Pikaboo", "Bluebell", "Mr. Macaroni" and the like don't sound like real-friend names.

I hereby name you Benrik!

Tuesday: Earn his affection.

Comb his hair. Get him a drink if he's thirsty. Save a seat for him on the bus and tell others not to sit there.

Ah! Where is that little fucker when I really need him!!!

Benrik! I've built you a nice house!

Benrik's house

This way in Benrik

Wednesday: Talk to him in public.

Gossip. Argue. Laugh at each other's jokes. You're buddies, and you don't care who knows it.

STOP

HAHA HAHAHAH AHAHAHAHA HAHAHAHAH HAHAHAHAH HAHAH

Thursday: Introduce him to everyone!

It's time to meet your other friends — and family. Don't be shy about it: if they like you they'll like him.

Excuse me, but don't think for a moment that I haven't noticed your refusal to say "Have a Merry Christmas" to my friend Benrik in front of me so I'm leaving goodbye!!!

Is he taking his medication?

Buddhist Fundamentalism Week

The Buddhist religion has so far failed to spawn a militant arm that would enforce their worldview against those of other more aggressive religions. We have corrected this anomaly by starting a Buddhist Fundamentalist group. Their eightfold demands are set out opposite. Join their armed struggle today on www.thiswebsitewillchangeyourlife.com.

1. Relax– or we kill you.

2. Through meditation let us annihilate our enemies.

3. Enlightenment at the barrel of a gun.

4. Go with the flow, or die, infidel.

5. You will be made to reach Nirvana, even if it's under torture.

6. All Buddhist suicide bombers to be reborn as Bill Gates.

7. The Middle Way or the highway.

8. Unless everyone chills out immediately, we slaughter them.

Buddhist Fundamentalism Week

Monday 24	Tuesday 25	Wednesday 26
9		
10		
11		
12		
13		
14		
15		
16		
17		
18		

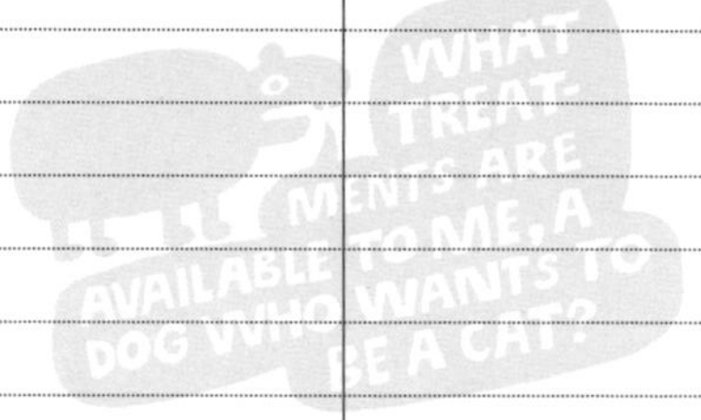

Thursday 27	
9	
10	
11	
12	
13	
14	
15	
16	
17	
18	

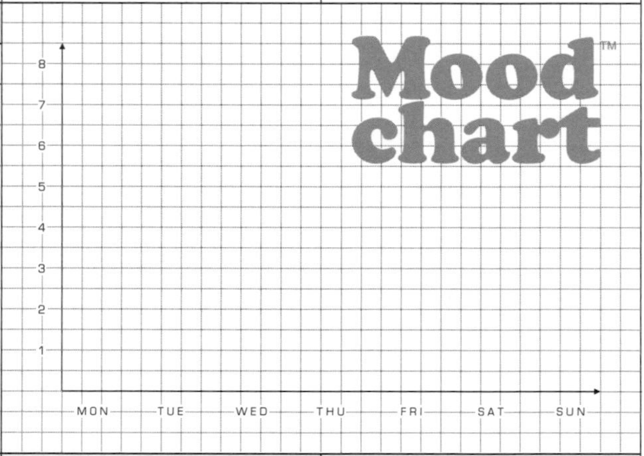

Mood chart ™

8
7
6
5
4
3
2
1

MON — TUE — WED — THU — FRI — SAT — SUN

Friday 28	Saturday 29	Sunday 30
9		
10		
11		
12		
13		
14		
15		
16		
17		
18		

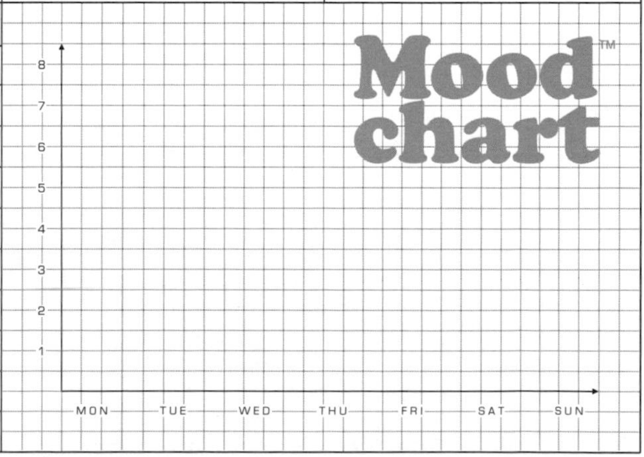

Rebel against your astrological sign

Monday 1 — MAY BANK HOLIDAY (UK)

9
10
11
12
13
14
15
16
17
18

Tuesday 2

9
10
11
12
13
14
15
16
17
18

Wednesday 3

9
10
11
12
13
14
15
16
17
18

Thursday 4

9
10
11
12
13
14
15
16
17
18

Friday 5

9
10
11
12
13
14
15
16
17
18

Saturday 6

9
10
11
12
13
14
15
16
17
18

Sunday 7

9
10
11
12
13
14
15
16
17
18

Mood chart™

8
7
6
5
4
3
2
1

MON — TUE — WED — THU — FRI — SAT — SUN

THIS WEEK REBEL AGAINST YOUR ASTROLOGICAL SIGN!

ARIES

TAURUS

GEMINI

CANCER

LEO

VIRGO

LIBRA

SCORPIO

SAGITTARIUS

CAPRICORN

AQUARIUS

PISCES

THIS WEEK, FAKE YOUR OWN
KIDNAPPING AND SEE IF
ANYONE PAYS THE RANSOM

HOW MUCH DO YOUR LOVED
ONES REALLY LOVE YOU?
Find out with this
harmless subterfuge.
Simply fill in this
pre-prepared note; knock
a few things over to make
it look like there was a
struggle; take yourself
off to a remote country
hotel for the week; watch
events unfold. Bonus: Not
only will you find out
if you're valued, but
you could also walk
away with a cool
tax-free $50,000!

INCREASING THE PRESSURE:
To make sure your threat
is taken seriously, send
the following body parts
as the week progresses.
MONDAY: Lock of your hair.
TUESDAY: Fingernail.
WEDNESDAY: Wisdom tooth.
THURSDAY: Front tooth.
FRIDAY: Little finger.
SATURDAY: Big toe.
SUNDAY: Appendix.
FOLLOWING MONDAY: Head
on a platter. Your
bluff has been called.

USE THESE SPECIAL BODY-PART-SENDING STAMPS!

We HAVE...................
NOthiNG WiLL HarM
HeR/hiM if $50,000
are Left HeRE:.........
.....................by
SAtuRDay at NOOn.
Do Not coNtact
the POLice or sHe/
he WiLL diE HOR-
riBLy. NO TriCKs!
SignEd:AnOnyMUs

Fake your own kidnapping

Monday 8	Tuesday 9	Wednesday 10
9		
10		
11		
12		
13		
14		
15		
16		
17		
18		

Thursday 11	
9	
10	
11	
12	
13	
14	
15	
16	
17	
18	

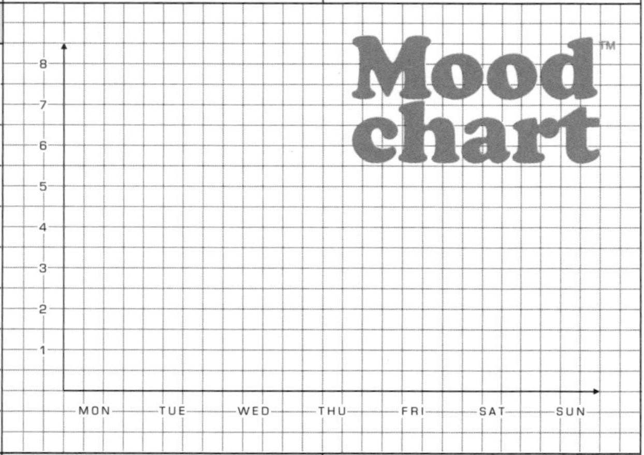

Mood chart™

8
7
6
5
4
3
2
1

MON — TUE — WED — THU — FRI — SAT — SUN

Friday 12	Saturday 13	Sunday 14
9		
10		
11		
12		
13		
14		
15		
16		
17		
18		

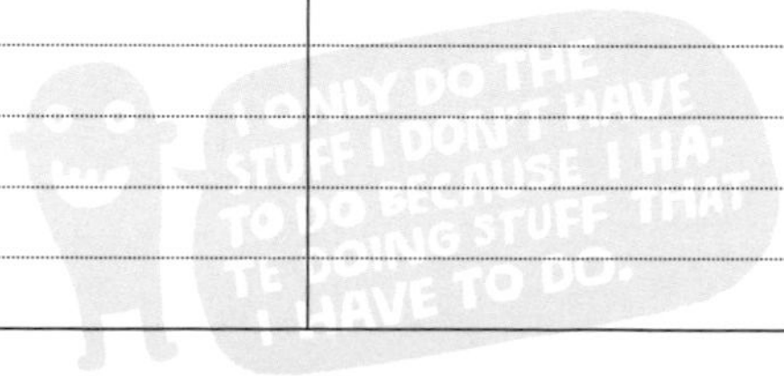

Monday 15	Tuesday 16	Wednesday 17
9		
10		
11		
12		
13		
14		
15		
16		
17		
18		

Thursday 18	Friday 19	Saturday 20
9		
10		
11		
12		
13		
14		
15		
16		
17		
18		

Sunday 21	
9	
10	
11	
12	
13	
14	
15	
16	
17	
18	

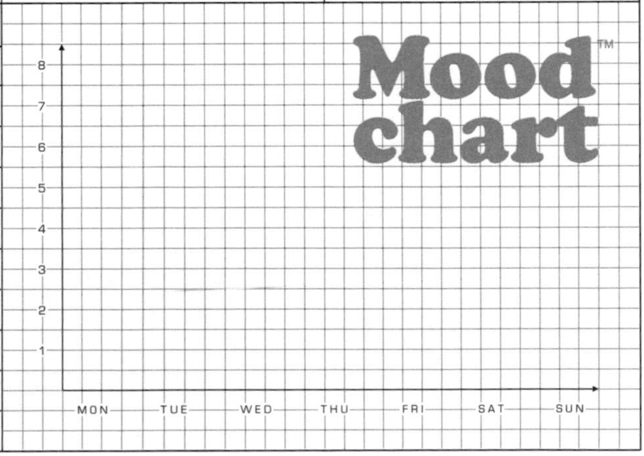

Aversion Diet Week

Mood chart™

8
7
6
5
4
3
2
1

MON — TUE — WED — THU — FRI — SAT — SUN

AVERSION DIET WEEK

Most diets are far too complicated. Carbohydrate content, GI indexes and other macrobiotic nonsense only make it less likely that the diet will be followed. This is why Benrik are introducing the new "Aversion Diet". The "Aversion Diet" works on a very basic principle: if you eat less, you'll lose weight. Simply open the Diary at this page, stare at these unappetizing images during mealtimes, and you are guaranteed results within the week.

MONDAY
Think of them on your flesh!

TUESDAY
Not pretty, is it?

WEDNESDAY
Yummy!

THURSDAY
Particularly good if
you're eating meat.

FRIDAY
It's OK to leave
food on your plate.

SATURDAY
Concentrate on
the furry bits...

SUNDAY
Bon appétit!

This week, play God with other peoples' lives

The village of Likabula is one of the poorest in Malawi, with roughly 100 villagers surviving on an average of $15/month. If every Diary reader donates £5 this week, the village will be rich, and you will have changed the fortunes of an entire community. Go on, play God.

Likabula

Population: 104
Language: Chichewa/English
Currency: Kwacha
Religion: Christian
Economy: Tea, Mt Mulanje guiding, forestry
Life expectancy: 37

MAY 22 28

2006

Benrikville

Send cheque made out to "Benrik Likabula Fund",
c/o Benrik Limited, PFD, Drury House, 34-43 Russell St, London
WC2B 5HA, UK. It's for charity, so it's compulsory!

Play God with other peoples' lives

Monday 22	Tuesday 23	Wednesday 24
9		
10		
11		
12		
13		
14		
15		
16		
17		
18		

Thursday 25	
9	
10	
11	
12	
13	
14	
15	
16	
17	
18	

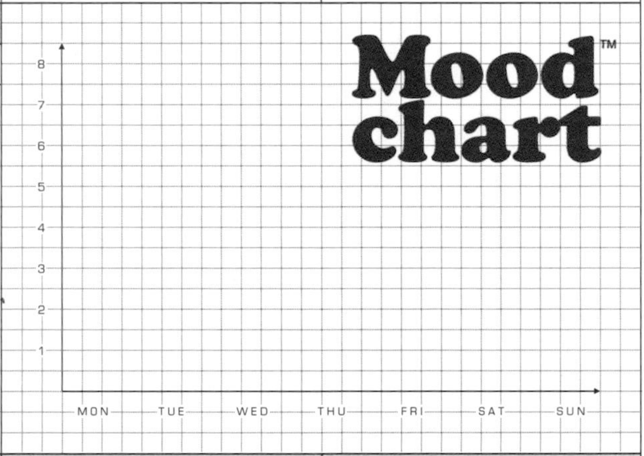

Mood chart ™

8
7
6
5
4
3
2
1

MON — TUE — WED — THU — FRI — SAT — SUN

Friday 26	Saturday 27	Sunday 28
9		
10		
11		
12		
13		
14		
15		
16		
17		
18		

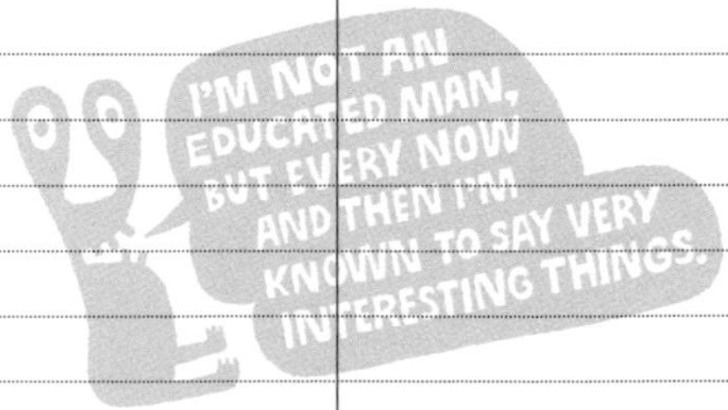

I'M NOT AN EDUCATED MAN, BUT EVERY NOW AND THEN I'M KNOWN TO SAY VERY INTERESTING THINGS.

Monday 29	Tuesday 30	Wednesday 31
9		
10		
11		
12		
13		
14		
15		
16		
17		
18		

Thursday 1	Friday 2	Saturday 3
9		
10		
11		
12		
13		
14		
15		
16		
17		
18		

Sunday 4	
9	
10	
11	
12	
13	
14	
15	
16	
17	
18	

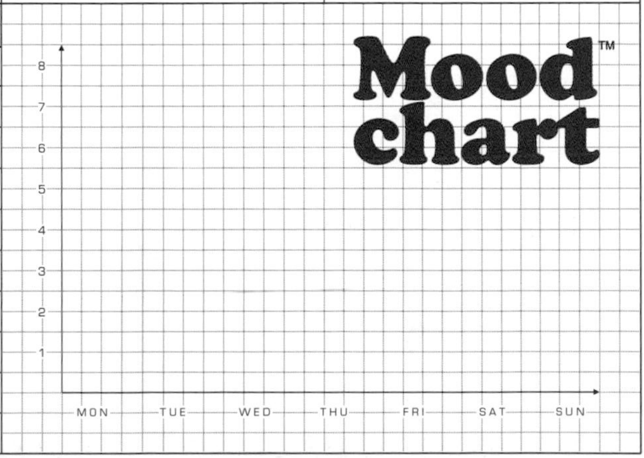

Lend your mobile to a homeless person

Mood™ chart

8
7
6
5
4
3
2
1

MON — TUE — WED — THU — FRI — SAT — SUN

This week, lend your mobile to a homeless person and ask them to take your calls, screening out anyone they don't like the sound of.

Important Message!

Date.................... Time............... A.m. ☐ P.m. ☐
Caller..
Of...
Phone number...

Telephoned   ☐   Will call again   ☐
Returned your call ☐   Wishes to see you   ☐
Please call   ☐

Response: They're busy!   ☐
            They're dead!   ☐
            They hate you!   ☐
            Fuck off!   ☐
            Can I take a message?   ☐

Important Message!

Date.................... Time............... A.m. ☐ P.m. ☐
Caller..
Of...
Phone number...

Telephoned   ☐   Will call again   ☐
Returned your call ☐   Wishes to see you   ☐
Please call   ☐

Response: They're busy!   ☐
            They're dead!   ☐
            They hate you!   ☐
            Fuck off!   ☐
            Can I take a message?   ☐

Important Message!

Date.................... Time............... A.m. ☐ P.m. ☐
Caller..
Of...
Phone number...

Telephoned   ☐   Will call again   ☐
Returned your call ☐   Wishes to see you   ☐
Please call   ☐

Response: They're busy!   ☐
            They're dead!   ☐
            They hate you!   ☐
            Fuck off!   ☐
            Can I take a message?   ☐

Important Message!

Date.................... Time............... A.m. ☐ P.m. ☐
Caller..
Of...
Phone number...

Telephoned   ☐   Will call again   ☐
Returned your call ☐   Wishes to see you   ☐
Please call   ☐

Response: They're busy!   ☐
            They're dead!   ☐
            They hate you!   ☐
            Fuck off!   ☐
            Can I take a message?   ☐

Important Message!

Date........................Time....................A.m. ☐ P.m. ☐
Caller...
Of...
Phone number...

Telephoned   ☐   Will call again   ☐
Returned your call   ☐   Wishes to see you   ☐
Please call   ☐

Response: They're busy!   ☐
            They're dead!   ☐
            They hate you!   ☐
            Fuck off!   ☐
            Can I take a message?   ☐

Important Message!

Date........................Time....................A.m. ☐ P.m. ☐
Caller...
Of...
Phone number...

Telephoned   ☐   Will call again   ☐
Returned your call   ☐   Wishes to see you   ☐
Please call   ☐

Response: They're busy!   ☐
            They're dead!   ☐
            They hate you!   ☐
            Fuck off!   ☐
            Can I take a message?   ☐

Important Message!

Date........................Time....................A.m. ☐ P.m. ☐
Caller...
Of...
Phone number...

Telephoned   ☐   Will call again   ☐
Returned your call   ☐   Wishes to see you   ☐
Please call   ☐

Response: They're busy!   ☐
            They're dead!   ☐
            They hate you!   ☐
            Fuck off!   ☐
            Can I take a message?   ☐

Important Message!

Date........................Time....................A.m. ☐ P.m. ☐
Caller...
Of...
Phone number...

Telephoned   ☐   Will call again   ☐
Returned your call   ☐   Wishes to see you   ☐
Please call   ☐

Response: They're busy!   ☐
            They're dead!   ☐
            They hate you!   ☐
            Fuck off!   ☐
            Can I take a message?   ☐

This week, put yourself up for

Tips to help you sell yourself

Include a photo. No one will be interested in buying you unless they can see what you look like. Make sure the photo is a recent one. No naked photos, unless you are looking to be sold as a sex slave.

Give a description. As eBay themselves advise, "give some thought to describing your item. What are its most appealing characteristics?" Be specific: "proficient at computer software installation including Windows XP and Mac OSX" beats "easygoing".

Choose the right category. The right category is: Everything Else > Weird Stuff > Slightly Unusual.

Pick a realistic starting price. Research shows that £100 is all that most people are prepared to bid initially for an average human being. Unless you are beautiful or famous, start at £100 and work your way up through the auction process.

sale on eBay!

Let us know the result. Benrik are interested in your well-being, wish to follow your progress, and will claim their 10% off your eventual price.

Monday 5	Tuesday 6	Wednesday 7
9		
10		
11		
12		
13		
14		
15		
16		
17		
18		

Thursday 8

| 9 |
| 10 |
| 11 |
| 12 |
| 13 |
| 14 |
| 15 |
| 16 |
| 17 |
| 18 |

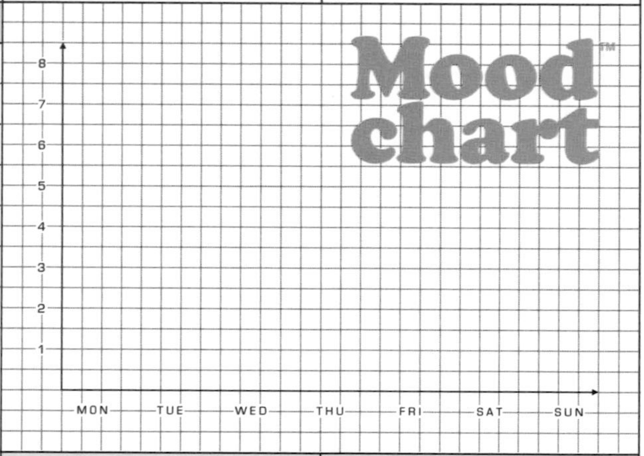

Mood chart™

8
7
6
5
4
3
2
1

MON — TUE — WED — THU — FRI — SAT — SUN

Friday 9	Saturday 10	Sunday 11
9		
10		
11		
12		
13		
14		
15		
16		
17		
18		

Monday 12	Tuesday 13	Wednesday 14
9		
10		
11		
12		
13		
14		
15		
16		
17		
18		

Thursday 15	Friday 16	Saturday 17
9		
10		
11		
12		
13		
14		
15		
16		
17		
18		

Sunday 18	
9	
10	
11	
12	
13	
14	
15	
16	
17	
18	

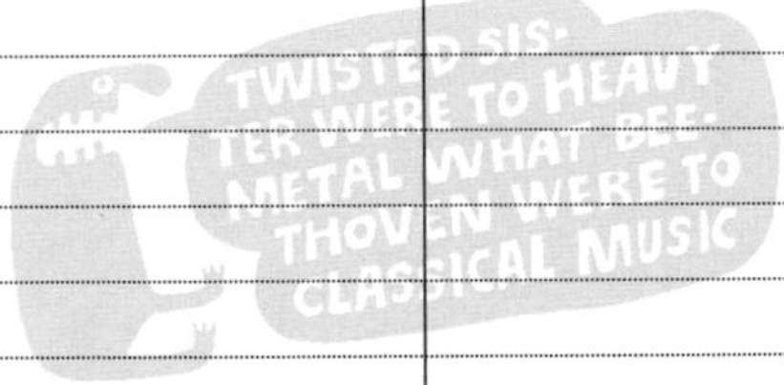

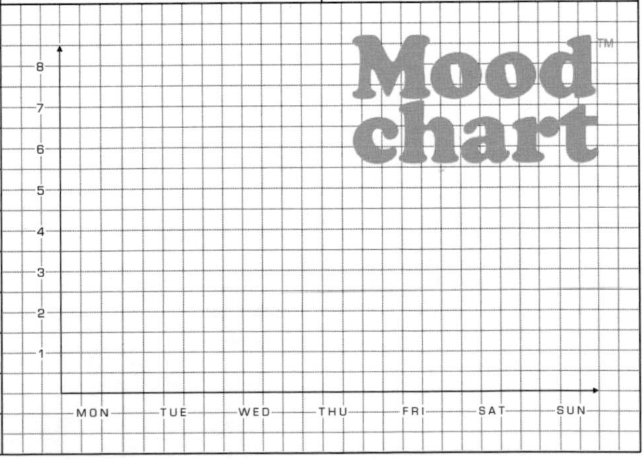

Mood chart

MON TUE WED THU FRI SAT SUN

This week, have a row with everyone you meet

Let off steam with this extreme stress-relief method. It's easy: you can start a row over anything, from rip-off taxi fares to rubbish collectors not doing their job properly. Start with insolence, and build up to a nuclear rage. Refuse to see sense!

Reasonableness is the chloroform of our times, the mental cage from which we dare not escape. It is permanent compromise, which only hormone-addled teenagers and mad poets may challenge. This week, revolt against sensibleness: with everyone you meet, rage, burn and rave!

Sorry!

Why don't you get a job instead of begging?

I know I'm 103 but I'm not ready to die yet, so fuck off with that stupid scythe.

That light wasn't red, officer.

I didn't step on your foot, you must have dreamt it.

I feel a lot healthier since I started smoking, doctor.

Ecumenical Week: Try out all major

Religion	History	Beliefs	Sacred text	Logo	Slogan
Monday	Founded by Siddartha Gautama (the Buddha) in the 5th century BC in what is now Nepal, Buddhism spread across much of Asia in the centuries following his death.	There is no God; we go through a succession of reincarnations, with our past actions influencing our next life. The cycle can be halted by reaching enlightenment (nirvana), essentially through meditation and the Middle Way.	The Tri-Pitaka.		"To avoid all that is evil, to cultivate what is good, to purify the mind."
Tuesday	Hinduism is one of the world's oldest religions, originating over 3000 years ago near the river Indus, with complex roots and no single human founder.	There is a universal God or soul called Brahman, who is also expressed in the form of deities such as Krishna, Vishnu, Shiva, and Rama. Life is a great cycle of birth, death and rebirth, governed by Karma, the law of cause and effect.	The Bhagavad Gita, The Upanishads.		"The mind of man is the root of both bondage and release."
Wednesday	Modern paganism covers most of the ancestral pre-monotheistic religions of the world, from Celtic druidry to Native American shamanism.	Nature and Mother Earth are spiritual, and are to be respected and worshipped, often in the guise of individual gods. The divine in nature has a strong feminine side, linked to the renewal and rebirth of the seasons.	The Golden Bough (Sir James George Frazer).		"The Earth is our Mother and we must take care of her."
Thursday	Atheism is a relatively recent creed. Although the Greeks hinted at it, it only really took off with the Enlightenment. In the 19th century, Darwin, Feuerbach and Nietzsche all contributed to its rapid spread. It is now the unofficial religion of the West.	There are no gods. Faith is mere superstition to comfort the feeble-minded and/or prop up oppressive power systems.	Thus Spake Zarathustra (Nietzsche).		"God is dead."
Friday	Founded by the Prophet Muhammad in the 7th century after a direct revelation from Allah, Islam swiftly spread both west (all the way to Spain) and east (all the way to China).	Allah is the one and only God. Islam was revealed to humanity by Muhammad, Allah's last prophet. We must obey the Qu'ran and surrender ourselves to Allah.	The Qu'ran.		"There is no God but Allah, and Muhammad is his messenger."
Saturday	Judaism was founded 3500 years ago by Abraham and Moses – who led the Jewish people from Egyptian captivity to the Promised Land of Israel. Judaism has since accompanied the Jewish people in their dramatic history of exiles, persecutions and other tribulations.	There is only one God. The Jews are his chosen people.	The Torah.		"Hear O Israel, the Lord our God, the Lord is One."
Sunday	Founded by Jesus Christ, persecuted and crucified by the Romans for his heretical views. Said to have risen from the dead. Word spread by his apostles, including Paul. Christians persecuted until Roman emperor Constantine converted in 312 CE.	Jesus is the son of God, sent by him to redeem humanity. He was crucified for our sins but rose from the dead to join God in heaven.	The Bible.		"Love Thy Neighbour As Thyself."

Rituals	Entry requirements	Commitment level	Popular appeal	How to try it out	Your rating
These vary according to the different traditions, but meditation and some chanting are usually in order.	Acceptance of the Four Noble Truths, The Eight Fold Path and the Five Precepts.	Medium. Risk of being reborn as a beetle of some description.	350 million adherents worldwide, and an increasing influence on the Western popular worldview.	Sit in the lotus position for one hour with your eyes closed and your body relaxed, and focus solely on your breathing.	10
Offerings to the Gods, recitation of the Vedas, oblations, chanting of mantras.	Belief in the Vedas, in karma, dharma, and reincarnation. Being renamed (namakarana samskara).	Medium to high, depending on your caste.	Big in India of course. Appeal elsewhere restricted by its deep integration into Indian society, and by the bewildering variety of subgods.	Worship at your local Hindu temple today.	10
Music, prayer, dance, conducted in sacred circles outdoors on hilltops, in caves, near large stones.	Willingness to participate in communal outdoor rituals.	Medium-high. Requires a high tolerance of public ridicule and/or accusations of deviant sexual practices.	Limited. Although neo-paganism has seen a resurgence, partly fuelled by the growth in ecological awareness, it is still a niche religion with a PR problem.	Head for Stonehenge tonight and join in the Summer Solstice celebrations.	10
May adopt watered-down versions of other religions' rituals (weddings, funerals, Christmas).	None.	Used to involve being burnt at the stake. Now less risky.	Widespread. Most atheists are happy to just dismiss the whole religion thing, and hope like hell they don't turn out to be wrong.	Look up at the night sky tonight and imagine us alone, quite alone.*	10
The five pillars of Islam are: 1) Shahada (declaration of faith) 2) Salat (prayer five times a day) 3) Zakat (giving to charity every year) 4) Sawm (fasting during Ramadan) 5) Hajj (pilgrimage to Mecca at least once in a lifetime).	Open to all who believe sincerely in its teachings. Reciting the Shahada three times in front of witnesses is all that is formally required to become a Muslim.	High. Islam requires more visible worship than most religions.	Over a billion adherents make it the second most popular faith in the world. Also the fastest-growing.	Attend Friday prayers at your local mosque today.	10
Too numerous to detail.	Being or becoming Jewish. To become Jewish: find a sympathetic rabbi, study Judaism, get circumcised if you are a man, appear before the Bet Din (ritual court), choose a Hebrew name, go to the mikveh (ritual bath).	High. Orthodox Judaism pervades everyday life.	Limited, as Judaism is not a proselytising faith.	Visit the synagogue today.	10
Baptism, Confirmation, Eucharist.	Belief in Jesus as our saviour. Baptism.	High in theory, variable in practice.	Most popular faith in the world, with over 2 billion followers.	Go to church today.	10

(*although refer to the week of October 9)

Monday 19	Tuesday 20	Wednesday 21
9		
10		
11		
12		
13		
14		
15		
16		
17		
18		

Thursday 22

| 9 |
| 10 |
| 11 |
| 12 |
| 13 |
| 14 |
| 15 |
| 16 |
| 17 |
| 18 |

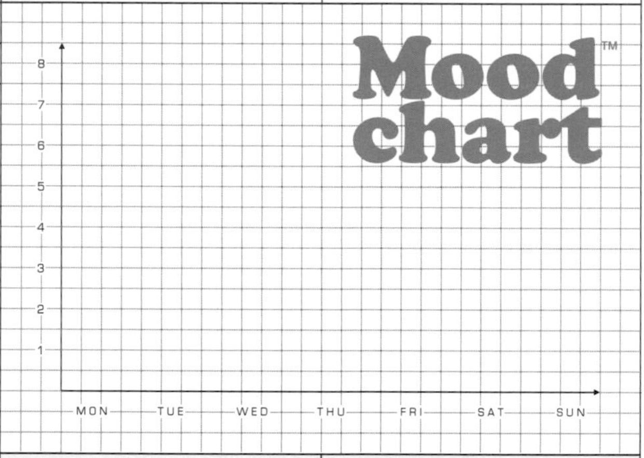

Mood chart™

8
7
6
5
4
3
2
1

MON — TUE — WED — THU — FRI — SAT — SUN

Friday 23	Saturday 24	Sunday 25
9		
10		
11		
12		
13		
14		
15		
16		
17		
18		

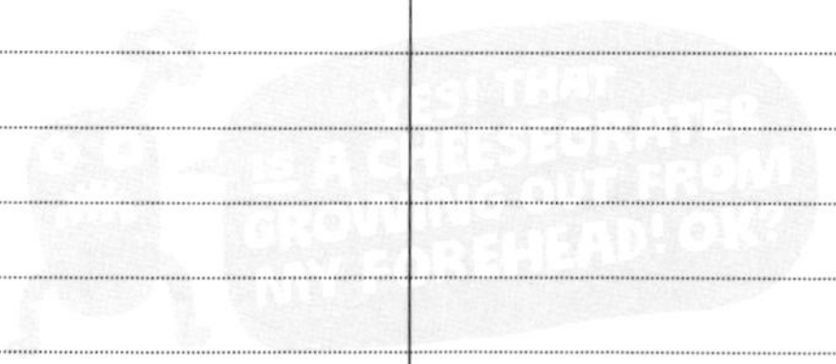

Act like you're invisible

Monday 26	Tuesday 27	Wednesday 28
9		
10		
11		
12		
13		
14		
15		
16		
17		
18		

Thursday 29	Friday 30	Saturday 1
9		
10		
11		
12		
13		
14		
15		
16		
17		
18		

Sunday 2
9
10
11
12
13
14
15
16
17
18

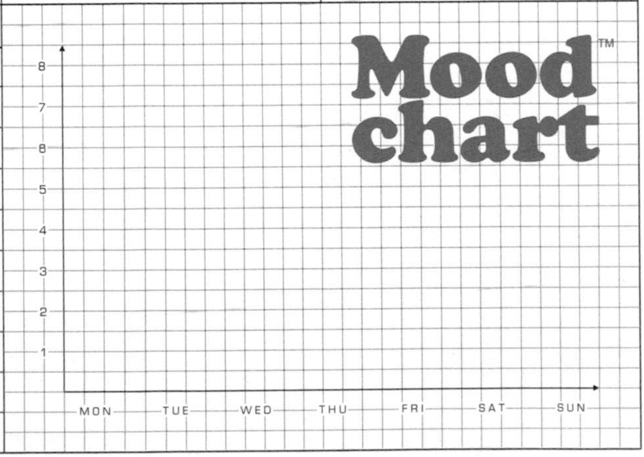

Mood™ chart

8
7
6
5
4
3
2
1

MON — TUE — WED — THU — FRI — SAT — SUN

Collective task: on Thursday at 10am, everyone gather in the Assyrian section of the British Museum (Room 6) and strip naked the first French tourist you

This week, act like you're invisible

Experience one of mankind's oldest moral quandaries: what would you do if you could get away with anything? Plato tells the tale of Gyges, shepherd to the King of Lydia, who finds a golden ring that confers invisibility on he who wears it. As soon as he realizes his power, Gyges goes to the court where he sleeps with the Queen and assassinates the King, taking his place. You may not want to go quite as far, but explore your hold on justice nonetheless. Would you steal, grope, murder? As ever, Benrik's legal disclaimer applies...

This week, insure your best feature.

Since Hollywood star Betty Grable insured her legs for $1m in the 1940s, actors and models have rushed to Lloyds of London to get their favourite body parts covered. Why shouldn't you? Call them for a quote on your finest asset on 020 7327 5448. Here is a rough guide to what you can expect to pay.

Nose (crooked)
Value: £167
Premium:
£3.65/month

Nose (cute)
Value: £5,890
Premium:
£54.03/month

Smile
Value: £1,845
Premium:
£23/month

Brain
Value: £54,000
Premium:
£231.65/month

Giant cock
Value: £21,780
Premium:
£359.70/month

Hairy hands
Value: £251
Premium:
£7.88/month

Suckable big toes
Value: £3,208
Premium:
£39.75/month

Je ne sais quoi
Value: £25,709
Premium:
£158.42/month

Personality
Value: £7
Premium:
£0.55/month

Insure your best feature

Monday 3	Tuesday 4	Wednesday 5
9		
10		
11		
12		
13		
14		
15		
16		
17		
18		

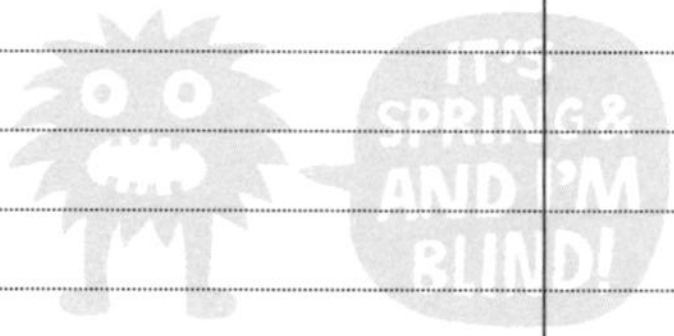

IT'S SPRING & AND I'M BLIND!

Thursday 6

9	
10	
11	
12	
13	
14	
15	
16	
17	
18	

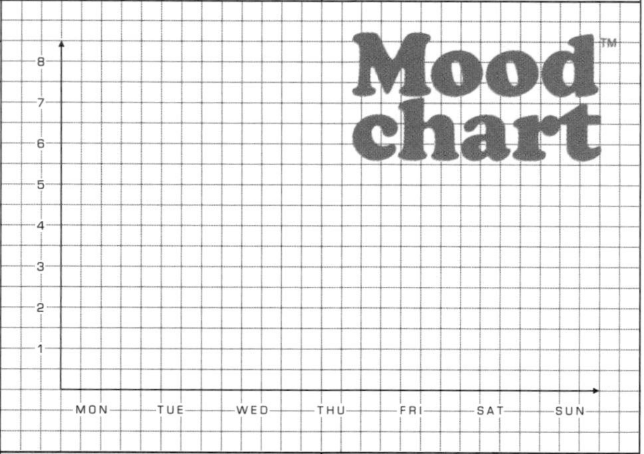

8
7
6
5
4
3
2
1

MON — TUE — WED — THU — FRI — SAT — SUN

Mood chart™

Friday 7	Saturday 8	Sunday 9
9		
10		
11		
12		
13		
14		
15		
16		
17		
18		

Monday 10	Tuesday 11	Wednesday 12
9		
10		
11		
12		
13		
14		
15		
16		
17		
18		

Thursday 13	Friday 14	Saturday 15
9		
10		
11		
12		
13		
14		
15		
16		
17		
18		

Sunday 16

| 9 |
| 10 |
| 11 |
| 12 |
| 13 |
| 14 |
| 15 |
| 16 |
| 17 |
| 18 |

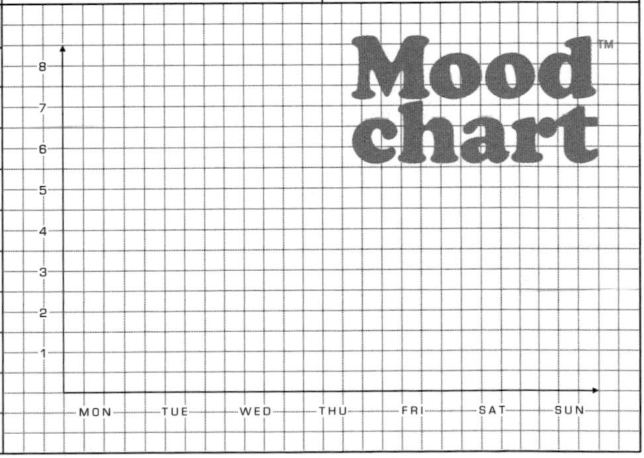

Mood chart™

8
7
6
5
4
3
2
1

MON — TUE — WED — THU — FRI — SAT — SUN

HOLIDAY
WEEK:

1. Run over a cow
British Consulate Emergency
Number +91 (11) 2419 2100

2. Tour the White House
in an "Osama Rules" T-shirt
British Consulate Emergency
Number +1 (202) 588 7800

3. Wear see-thru trousers
British Consulate Emergency
Number +966 (0) 1 488 0077

4. Attend a fancy-dress
party in SS uniform
British Consulate Emergency
Number +49 (30) 20457 579

5. Crack a Hiroshima joke
British Consulate Emergency
Number +81 (3) 5275 0346

CAUSE A DIPLOMATIC INCIDENT

Even the most unpatriotic citizens are somehow supposed to represent their country when they're abroad. Take advantage of your diplomatic aura this week, and commit a deliberately crass faux pas on behalf of your nation.

6. Stick chewing gum on government buildings
British Consulate Emergency Number +65 6424 4200

7. Ask where the coloured toilets are
British Consulate Emergency Number +27 (21) 405 2400

8. Carry a kilo of flour in your luggage
British Consulate Emergency Number +57 (1) 326 8300

As Freud revealed, dreams are the disguised fulfilment of repressed wishes. To deal with these repressed wishes, you may either undergo years of therapy, or you can act them out, thus confronting the problem at the root. This week, treat your dreams literally: make them happen...

Dream: "I was riding a goat naked, when I saw a penis-shaped cloud and fell off."

Repressed meaning: You are afraid of the animal nature of your sexuality. **Making it happen:** *Goat hire:* 020 7247 8764. *Riding breaks:* 024 7669 8300. *Meteorological Office:* 0870 900 0100. *Medical help:* 911.

Dream: "I'm standing on my head while Adolf Hitler whips me until I bleed."

Repressed meaning: Your hidden feelings of guilt are such that you cannot function in society. **Making it happen:** *Yoga lessons:* 01629 500991. *Dwarf dress hire:* www.simplyfancydress.co.uk. *Caution:* 020 8420 4209. *Plasters:* local pharmacist.

Dream: "All my teeth have been knocked out to help prop up the Great Wall of China."

Repressed meaning: You are worried about ageing, that your looks won't last for ever. **Making it happen:** *Dentist:* 020 7935 0875. *Chinese embassy:* 020 7299 4049. *Fedex:* 0800 123 800. *UN World Heritage Sites:* 00 1 212 963 9475.

Dream: "I'm a prisoner in a castle trying to let my hair down to escape, but the moat is full of babies."

Repressed meaning: You are having a midlife crisis. **Making it happen:** *Castle rentals:* 01573 229797. *Hair brooms:* www.tomandguy.co.uk. *Adoption agency:* 0800 783 4086. *Nappy wholesaler:* 0845 257 4658.

Dream: "The 747 I'm in flies into a flock of eagles and nearly crashes but I save the day."

Repressed meaning: You feel unrecognised by your work colleagues and hierarchical superiors. **Making it happen:** *Flying school:* 01980 674404. *Travel agent:* www.cheapflights.co.uk. *Animal rescue:* 020 3654 0459. *Life insurance:* 01603 622200.

Dream: "I'm being chased by a five-legged table into a field of squishy rotten pumpkins."

Repressed meaning: Your guess is as good as ours. **Making it happen:** *Furniture maker:* 01409 281767. *Costume hire association:* 0117 314 5000. *Trainers:* 0870 875 0500. *Magic mushrooms:* New Forest.

Make your dreams come true this week.

Bonus! Your wildest dream:
"Twelve high-class models are licking chocolate off my belly as I count my million-pound fortune."

Repressed meaning: You would quite like it if twelve high-class models licked chocolate off your belly as you counted your million-pound fortune. Making it happen: *Elite model agency* 00 1 212 529 9700, *The Chocolate Society:* 01423 322250, *National Lottery:* local newsagents, *Therapist:* 020 7267 3626.

Monday 17	Tuesday 18	Wednesday 19
9		
10		
11		
12		
13		
14		
15		
16		
17		
18		

Thursday 20		
9		
10		
11		
12		
13		
14		
15		
16		
17		
18		

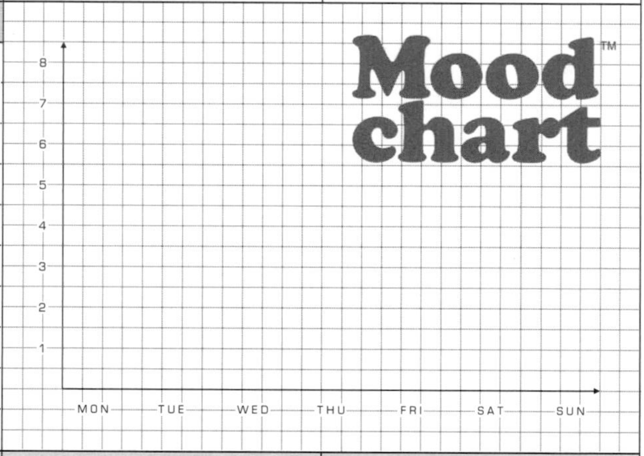

Mood chart™

8
7
6
5
4
3
2
1

MON — TUE — WED — THU — FRI — SAT — SUN

Friday 21	Saturday 22	Sunday 23
9		
10		
11		
12		
13		
14		
15		
16		
17		
18		

Stalk writers to become their muse

Monday 24	Tuesday 25	Wednesday 26
9		
10		
11		
12		
13		
14		
15		
16		
17		
18		

Thursday 27	Friday 28	Saturday 29
9		
10		
11		
12		
13		
14		
15		
16		
17		
18		

Sunday 30	
9	
10	
11	
12	
13	
14	
15	
16	
17	
18	

Mood chart ™

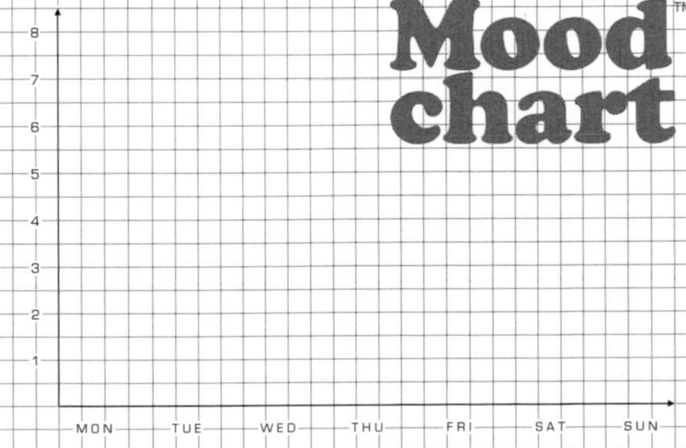

MON — TUE — WED — THU — FRI — SAT — SUN

8
7
6
5
4
3
2
1

This week, become a muse:
Stalk a well-known writer and

Will Self
Author of: *Great Apes, My Idea of Fun*
Lives: Stockwell
Look out for him: **Larkhall Park**

Suggested incident: **Impersonate a blind
pensioner who can only find his way home by
snorting a Hansel&Gretel-like line of cocaine
on the pavement all the way to the front door.**

Dan Brown
Author of: *The Da Vinci Code*
Lives: Exeter, New Hampshire
Look out for him: **Water St**

Suggested incident: **Paint blood-red stigmata
on your hands and smear them all over an
albino kitten before accomplices bundle you
into a blacked-out limo and speed off.**

Zadie Smith
Author of: *White Teeth, The Autograph Man*
Lives: Kilburn
Look out for her: **Willesden Lane**

Suggested incident: **Stage a fight between
Chinese, Pakistani and Jamaican men over
who is the real father of the gorgeous red-head
whose records were lost when the local sperm
donors clinic burnt down twenty years previous.**

JK Rowling
Author of: the *Harry Potter* series
Lives: Edinburgh
Look out for her: **Princes St**

Suggested incident: **Bite into an apple, then
shriek as you pull a handful of live worms
out of your pocket.**

set up a memorable incident that will inspire their next novel.

Salman Rushdie
Author of: *Midnight's Children, Satanic Verses*
Lives: New York
Look out for him: **Tribeca**

Suggested incident: **Offer to sell him the magic carpet that Ibn Battuta's great-great-granddaughter gave to your forebears in the year 1451, and on which he first flew over America, discovering it 100 years before Columbus.**

Martin Amis
Author of: *Money, London Fields*
Lives: Primrose Hill
Look out for him: **Regent's Park Road**

Suggested incident: **Dress up as a Gestapo officer in a heavy leather raincoat, and expose yourself to the children of hard-looking geezers until you get beaten to a pulp.**

Chuck Palahniuk
Author of: *Fight Club, Choke, Haunted*
Lives: Portland, Oregon
Look out for him: **Washington Park**

Suggested incident: **Accost a passer-by with a smile and claim you recognize them from your anger management class. Fly into a rage and headbutt them when they deny you've ever met.**

Benrik Ltd
Author of: *This Diary Will Change Your Life*
Lives: London
Look out for them: **Pretty much all over**

Suggested incident: **Throw fistfuls of banknotes at them, then run away.**

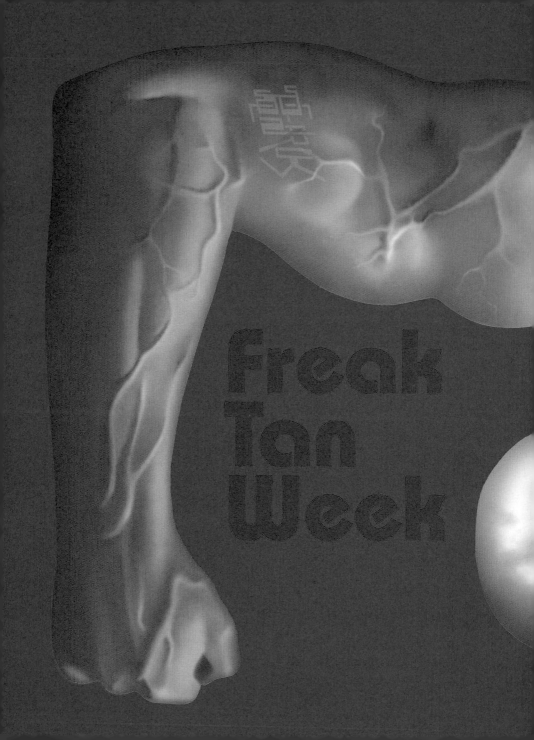

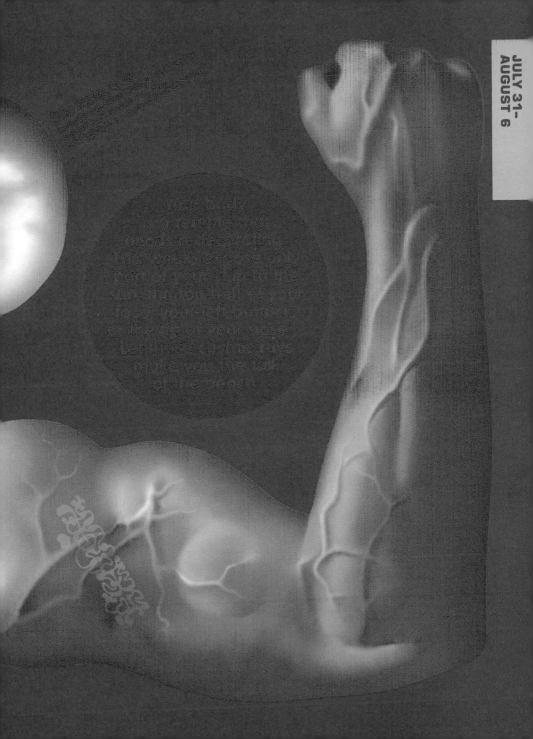

Your body
(and mind) now
needs re-decorating.
This week, expose EVERY
part of your skin to the
sun (just the half of your
face, your left buttock
or the tip of your nose.
Let those cosmic rays
make you the talk
of the beach.

Monday 31	Tuesday 1	Wednesday 2
9		
10		
11		
12		
13		
14		
15		
16		
17		
18		

Thursday 3		
9		
10		
11		
12		
13		
14		
15		
16		
17		
18		

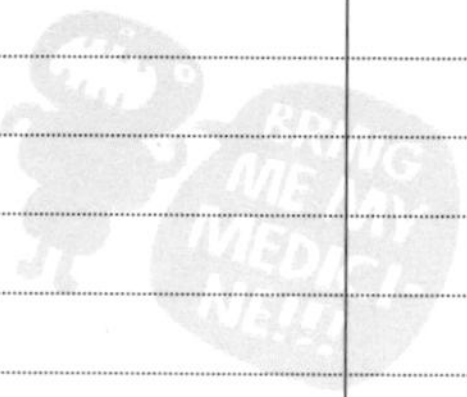

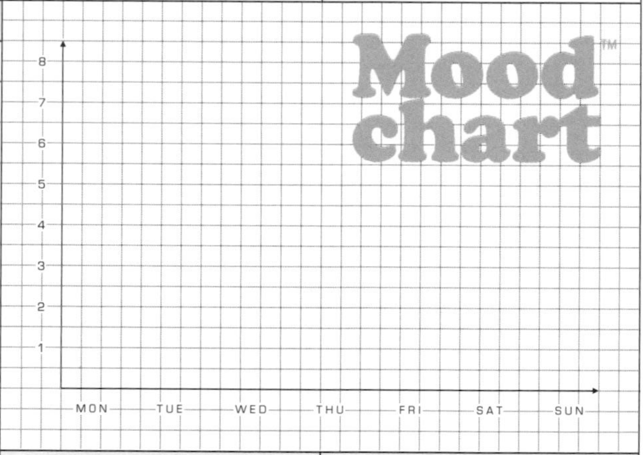

Mood chart™

MON TUE WED THU FRI SAT SUN

Friday 4	Saturday 5	Sunday 6
9		
10		
11		
12		
13		
14		
15		
16		
17		
18		

Run away as far as you can

Monday 7 BANK HOLIDAY (SCOTLAND)	Tuesday 8	Wednesday 9
9		
10		
11		
12		
13		
14		
15		
16		
17		
18		

Thursday 10	Friday 11	Saturday 12
9		
10		
11		
12		
13		
14		
15		
16		
17		
18		

Sunday 13	
9	
10	
11	
12	
13	
14	
15	
16	
17	
18	

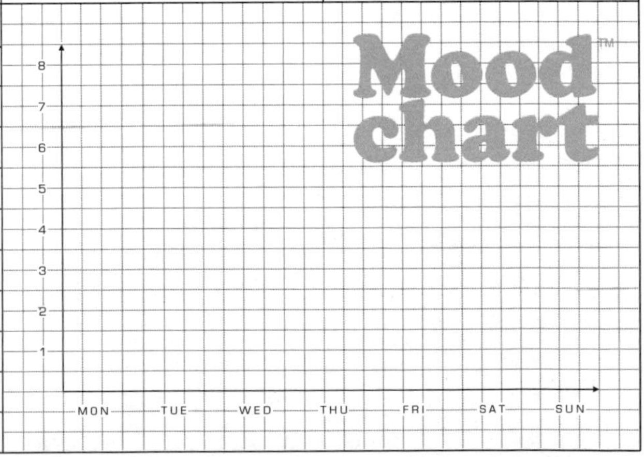

Mood™ chart

8
7
6
5
4
3
2
1

MON — TUE — WED — THU — FRI — SAT — SUN

(Based on 12 hours travelling per day for one week, starting in London, England.)

This week run away

Change your life by getting the hell away from it. See how far you can go in one week. Here we show the average speeds you should try to beat.

Running 10mph

Walking 4mph

Greetings from Luxembourg

This week, spark a political debate

This week, everyone using the Dia
a minor issue into a national pa
problem of dogshit. Write to the
radio talk shows, email TV news
MP and ask them to bring it up
Sunday, the Dogshit Dilemma sh
across the front pages and bring d
two. Dominate that media! The issu
dogshit is a national disgrace. By
we send out a message to societ
is acceptable, so please feel fre

Neighbourhood
PoopWatch

Do you know
the human
responsible for the
dog responsible for this
poop? If so, call our
anonymous 24-hour
hotline and denounce the
non-scoopers! 0800 767 6544.

Affix to pavement next to dogshit

issue encapsula
respect, anomi
urban disinteg
both corrosive
tolerance is the
must be DNA-
owners and the
and shamed. P
objects at www.

y must help spin
tical crisis: the
ewspapers, call
esks, lobby your
Parliament. By
uld be splashed
wn a minister or
e: The ubiquity of

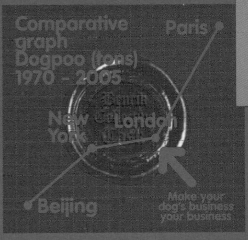

Comparative
graph
Dogpoo (tons)
1970 – 2005

Paris

New
York

London

Beijing

Make your
dog's business
your business

rting pet owners defile our streets,
as a whole: antisocial behaviour
to steal, rape and murder! The
es all others: carelessness, lack of
social disorder, political apathy,
ation. Small signs of decay are
f society and symptomatic. Zero
nly solution: any unscooped poop
nalysed and traced back to its
owners, who will then be named
st photographs of any offending
niswebsitewillchangeyourlife.com.

Spark a political debate

Monday 14	Tuesday 15	Wednesday 16
9		
10		
11		
12		
13		
14		
15		
16		
17		
18		

Thursday 17		
9		
10		
11		
12		
13		
14		
15		
16		
17		
18		

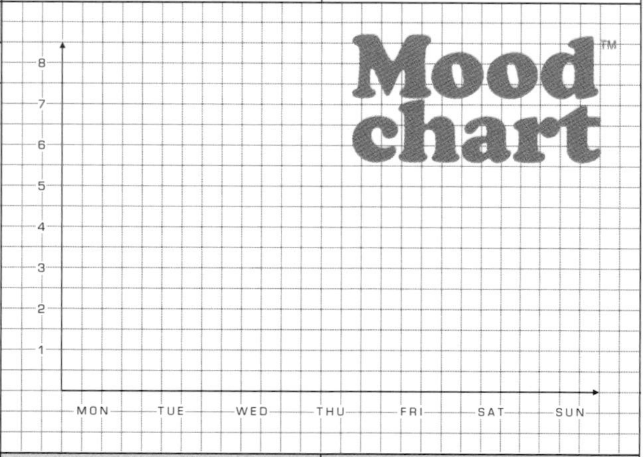

Mood chart ™

8
7
6
5
4
3
2
1

MON — TUE — WED — THU — FRI — SAT — SUN

Friday 18	Saturday 19	Sunday 20
9		
10		
11		
12		
13		
14		
15		
16		
17		
18		

Monday 21	BANK HOLIDAY (SCOTLAND)	Tuesday 22	Wednesday 23
9			
10			
11			
12			
13			
14			
15			
16			
17			
18			

Thursday 24	Friday 25	Saturday 26
9		
10		
11		
12		
13		
14		
15		
16		
17		
18		

YES, YOU GUESSED IT. THE GUY WHO WROTE THE SCORE FOR LEGALLY BLONDE...

Sunday 27

9
10
11
12
13
14
15
16
17
18

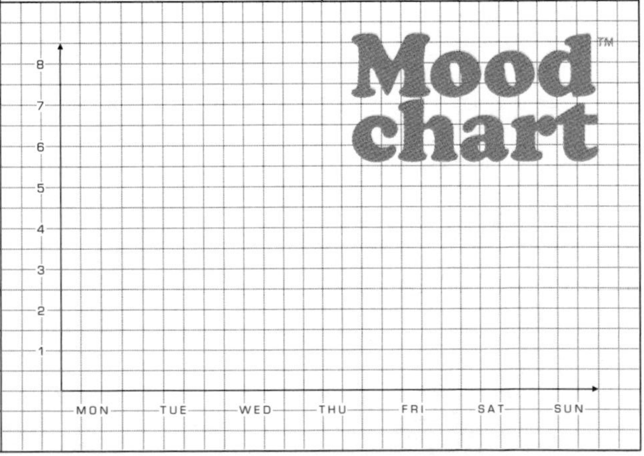

Mood chart™

8
7
6
5
4
3
2
1

MON — TUE — WED — THU — FRI — SAT — SUN

Add your touch to an artistic masterpiece this week

Velasquez

The idea that art is ever "finished" is thoroughly bourgeois. There's always room for improvement; indeed, without additional input, art can quickly fall behind the times. This week, visit your local museum, and update a fusty old exhibit.

B

Velasquez/Bettrik

MARRY A
BENRIK MAIL-ORDER
SPOUSE THIS WEEK!

MALE

TRISTAN MINIFIE

Age: 20
Gender: Male
Height: 6 ft
Weight: 125
Location: Little
Hampton, Australia

Food: Sweet and Sour Pork
Band: System of a Down
Colour: Yellow
GSOH: Yes
No. of wedding guests: 30
Requests: Must be Japanese

KEVIN ALBOROUGH

Age: 20
Gender: Male
Height: 5'11"
Weight: 150 lbs
Location: North Bay
Ontario, Canada

Food: Dang quesadilluhs
Band: Bright Eyes, Tom Waits
Colour: blue, black or green
GSOH: Yes
No. of wedding guests: 25
Requests: Girls preferred.

ANTE MILETIC

Age: 21
Gender: Male
Height: 6 feet
Weight: 165lbs
Location: Bellevue,
Washington, USA

Food: Sea
Band: Blood For Blood
Colour: Green
GSOH: Yes
No. of wedding guests: 3
Requests: No boys please

EMIL LARIN

Age: 28
Gender: Male
Height: 181 cm
Weight: 73kg
Location: New York
Food: Yam Nua

Band: Gershon Kingsley
Colour: Camouflage
GSOH: No
No. of wedding guests: ~50
Requests: No fucking star trek
or other uncool themes please

DOMINIC GOODRUM

Age: 25
Gender: Male
Height: 5ft8
Weight: 71kg
Location: Brighton,
United Kingdom

Food: Chile con carne
Band: Kings of Leon
Colour: Red
GSOH: yes
No. of wedding guests: 50-100
Requests: beautiful inside and out

JOEL MOSS LEVINSON

Age: 24
Gender: Male
Height: 5' 2"
Weight: 175-185
Location: Los Angeles, USA
Food: Steak

Band: Wilco, Colour: Blue
GSOH: Yes
No. of wedding guests:
The more the merrier
Requests: Straight,
English speaker, Jewish

XAVIER CARLIER

Age: 36
Gender: Male
Height: 174cm
Weight: 65kg
Location: Lyon, France
Food: cassoulet

Band: Telephone
Colour: Rainbow
GSOH: Yes
No. of wedding guests: 20ish
Requests: I would like my bride
not to be french, as I am already

THEO HARDEN

Age: 5
Gender: Male
Height: 1m10
Weight: 46kg
Location: Reading,
United Kingdom

Food: Chicken Nuggets
Band: Michael Jackson
Colour: Red and Yellow, GSOH: –
No. of wedding guests: 100 million!
Requests: Must be vetted by
little Theo's parents

ANDY SMOLICH

Age: 29
Gender: Male
Height: 184 cm
Weight: 92kg
Location: London,
United Kingdom

Food: red meat
Band: Iron Maiden
Colour: Black
GSOH: Yes
No. of wedding guests: 666
Requests: Must be ladylike

For mysterious reasons, many Benrik readers are single, even though their shared sense of humour makes them delightful and amusing life companions, with tremendous genetic potential. That is why Benrik encourage interbreeding amongst their fans. Here are a few that have asked Benrik to find them a spouse. Pick the one who takes your fancy, and email your choice to contact@benrik.co.uk. First come first served, so don't delay. Once your application is approved, Benrik will send you your spouse within 3 weeks.

*Don't see anyone you like? Register on www.thiswebsitewillchangeyourlife.com and we'll find you someone special too.

FEMALE

AMANDA YEE

Age: 22
Gender: Female
Height: 5'10
Weight: 145
Location: Charlotte, NC, USA.

Food: Thai or Greek
Band: Radiohead
Colour: Red
GSOH: Yes
No. of wedding guests: 200
Requests: DJ to play ghetto rap.

JEN BYRNE

Age: 21
Gender: Female
Height: 5'5"
Weight: 117
Location: Seattle, WA, USA

Food: Tangerines
Band: Death Cab For Cutie
Colour: Yellow
GSOH: Yes
No. of wedding guests: 20
Requests: No religion - I'm atheist.

GRACE JAO

Age: 19
Gender: Female
Height: 5'2
Weight: 180
Location: Quezon, Philippines

Food: lamb
Band: maroon 5
Colour: black
GSOH: Yes
No. of wedding guests: 38
Requests: Speak in english

DIMITY VANDERPOT

Age: 22
Gender: Female
Height: 165cm
Weight: 55/60kg
Location: Sydney, Australia

Food: strawberries
Band: Coldplay
Colour: aqua and ultramarine blue
GSOH: Yes
No. of wedding guests: 72
Requests: Speak english please

ROXANN JAPPIE

Age: 20
Gender: Female
Height: 5'10"
Weight: 60kg
Location: Kent, UK
Food: Pizza

Band: Weezer
Colour: yellow
GSOH: Yes
No. of wedding guests: 2
Requests: We will need to have a big piss up after the wedding

LAURA LORTIE

Age: 18
Gender: Female
Height: 5'7
Weight: 130
Location: Sudbury, Canada
Food: razzn gizzle

Band: Dashboard Confessional
Colour: Brown
GSOH: Yes
No. of wedding guests: who ever shows up
Requests: english all the way

JOHANNA HJELM

Age: 19
Gender: Female
Height: 163 cm
Weight: 60 k
Location: Malmø, Sweden

Food: tex max
Band: beastie boys
Colour: black
GSOH: Yes
No. of wedding guests: 4
Requests: swedish or english speaking

ANNIE LANGENFELD

Age: 20
Gender: Female
Height: 5'7
Weight: 145
Location: Minneapolis, USA

Food: Pizza
Band: Modest Mouse
Colour: Brown
GSOH: Yes
No. of wedding guests: 20
Requests: -

LIZ MILLER

Age: 18
Gender: Female
Height: 5'0
Weight: 128
Location: Oyster Bay, USA

Food: girl scout cookies
Band: the matches
Colour: green
GSOH: Yes
No. of wedding guests: not sure
Requests: tall get me

Marry a Benrik mail-order spouse

Monday 28	Tuesday 29	Wednesday 30
9		
10		
11		
12		
13		
14		
15		
16		
17		
18		

Thursday 31

9	
10	
11	
12	
13	
14	
15	
16	
17	
18	

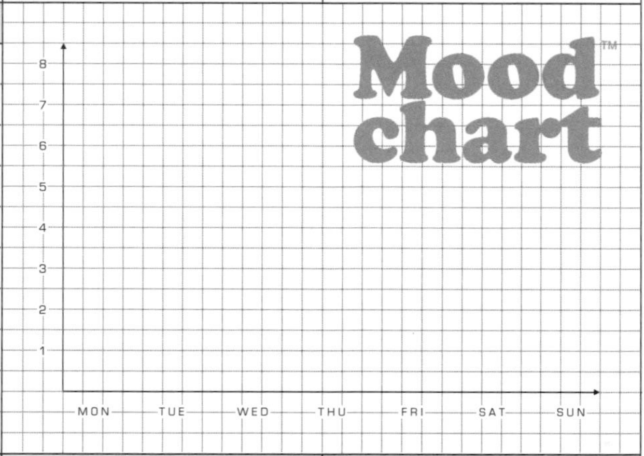

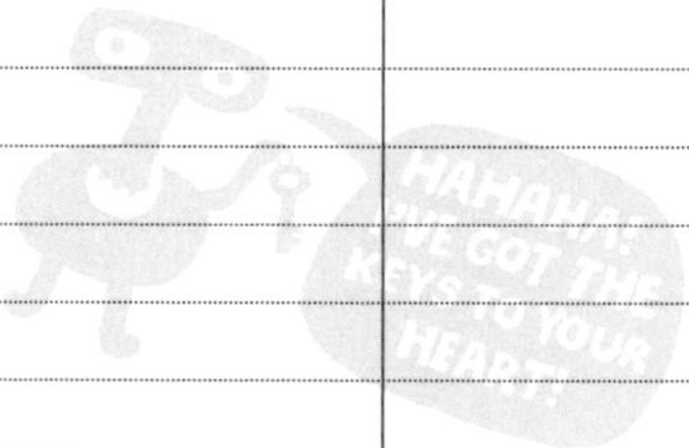

Mood chart™

8
7
6
5
4
3
2
1

MON — TUE — WED — THU — FRI — SAT — SUN

Friday 1	Saturday 2	Sunday 3
9		
10		
11		
12		
13		
14		
15		
16		
17		
18		

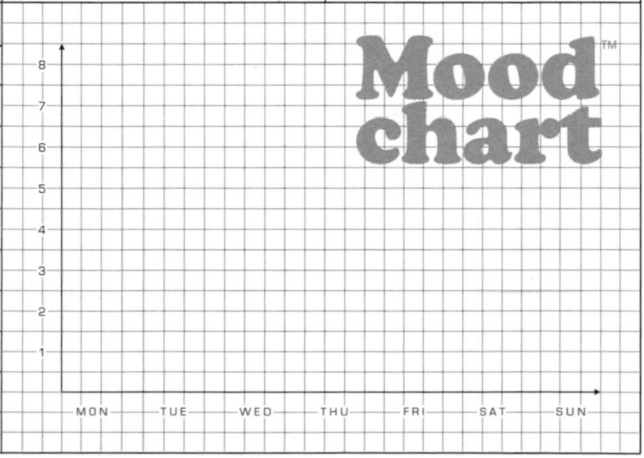

Assess people's potential for evil and act in consequence

Monday 4	BANK HOLIDAY (SCOTLAND)	Tuesday 5	Wednesday 6
9			
10			
11			
12			
13			
14			
15			
16			
17			
18			

Thursday 7	Friday 8	Saturday 9
9		
10		
11		
12		
13		
14		
15		
16		
17		
18		

Sunday 10

9
10
11
12
13
14
15
16
17
18

Mood chart™

8
7
6
5
4
3
2
1

MON — TUE — WED — THU — FRI — SAT — SUN

This week, assess people's potential for evil and act in consequence.

Name: A. Hitler
Potential for evil: 10/10
Proof of potential: Mein Kampf
Confirmed by independent observer: Yes ☒ No ☐

Adolf Hitler outlined his plans for the Jewish people in *Mein Kampf*, published in 1923. If someone then had taken him seriously enough and killed him pre-emptively, millions of deaths would have been averted. Today, probe those around you for murderous designs, and, should you find any, take history into your own hands.

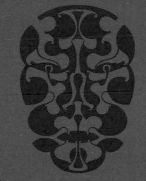

Name:........**Becky Montagu**..........
Potential for evil:......**9/10**............
Proof of potential:..**she fancies my Kevin**
Confirmed by independent observer: Yes ☐ No ☑

Name:...
Potential for evil:.........................
Proof of potential:.........................
Confirmed by independent observer: Yes ☐ No ☐

Name:...
Potential for evil:.........................
Proof of potential:.........................
Confirmed by independent observer: Yes ☐ No ☐

Name:...
Potential for evil:.........................
Proof of potential:.........................
Confirmed by independent observer: Yes ☐ No ☐

Name:...
Potential for evil:.........................
Proof of potential:.........................
Confirmed by independent observer: Yes ☐ No ☐

Name:...
Potential for evil:.........................
Proof of potential:.........................
Confirmed by independent observer: Yes ☐ No ☐

Name:...
Potential for evil:.........................
Proof of potential:.........................
Confirmed by independent observer: Yes ☐ No ☐

Name:...
Potential for evil:.........................
Proof of potential:.........................
Confirmed by independent observer: Yes ☐ No ☐

Name:...
Potential for evil:.........................
Proof of potential:.........................
Confirmed by independent observer: Yes ☐ No ☐

Plagiarism Week
This week, copy everything from others: your haircut, what you wear, where you go, what you say, what you read, what you watch, what you think.
My favourite film is Batman II.
Purple is the new black.
I think it's going to rain.
I've made salmon for dinner!
I'm worried my son is gay.
I love what you're wearing.
Voff!
I'm going on holiday with my husband to Venice.

Plagiarism Week
This week, copy everything from others: your haircut, what you wear, where you go, what you say, what you read, what you watch, what you think.
I have never seen a finer movie than Batman II.
Mauve is the new black.
Looks like rain to me!
Tonight's supper is fish-based!
Your choice of clothes is divine.
My boy is homosexual, what can I do?
Vaff!
Your husband and I are off to Venice, and you're staying here, biatch!

Monday 11	Tuesday 12	Wednesday 13
9		
10		
11		
12		
13		
14		
15		
16		
17		
18		

Thursday 14		
9		
10		
11		
12		
13		
14		
15		
16		
17		
18	MON TUE WED THU FRI SAT SUN	

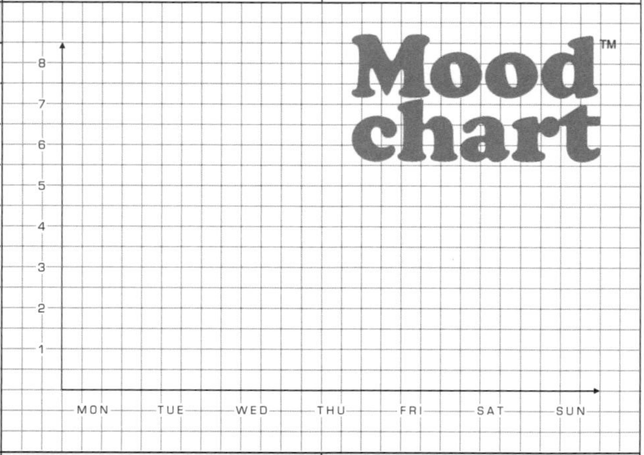

8
7
6
5
4
3
2
1

Mood™ chart

Friday 15	Saturday 16	Sunday 17
9		
10		
11		
12		
13		
14		
15		
16		
17		
18		

Monday 18	Tuesday 19	Wednesday 20
9		
10		
11		
12		
13		
14		
15		
16		
17		
18		

Thursday 21	Friday 22	Saturday 23
9		
10		
11		
12		
13		
14		
15		
16		
17		
18		

Sunday 24
9
10
11
12
13
14
15
16
17
18

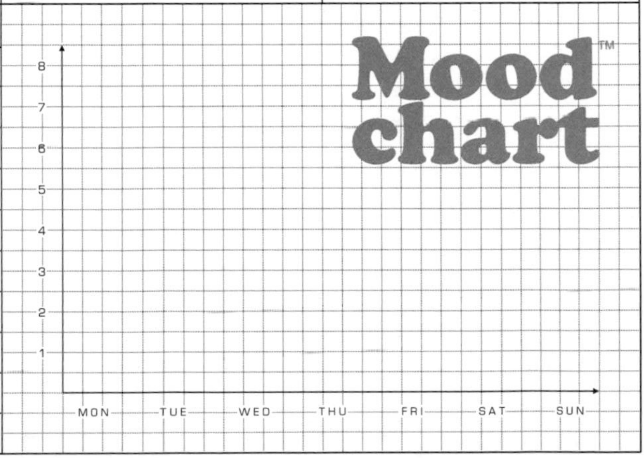

Live like you're in a commercial

Mood™ chart

8
7
6
5
4
3
2
1

MON — TUE — WED — THU — FRI — SAT — SUN

THIS WEEK, LIVE LIKE YOU'RE IN A COMMERCIAL

As you walk down the street, toss your hair as if you'd just stepped out of a salon. High five your colleagues during business meetings. Break into your neighbour's house and leave a box of chocolates on the table, and all because the lady loves Milk Tray. After eating any kind of foodstuff, examine the packaging again and say "mmmmm!"

Whilst in the bath, give blow jobs to bars of chocolate. Go to McDonald's and croon "I'm lovin' it" as you order a Big Mac. Dance or break into song after consuming sugary drinks. And ladies: if your period is due, be sure to go skydiving, paragliding and/or bungee jumping.

The Power of Advertising

Why not use it to your advantage by advertising yourself? Pick your most attractive trait, write it up as a slogan, and stick it in phone boxes, on trees, through letterboxes. Don't forget to include a photo and your phone number. Now sit back and see what happens.

TEST THE NATION WEEK

This week, go somewhere with lots of people, and fall over to see if anyone helps you up.

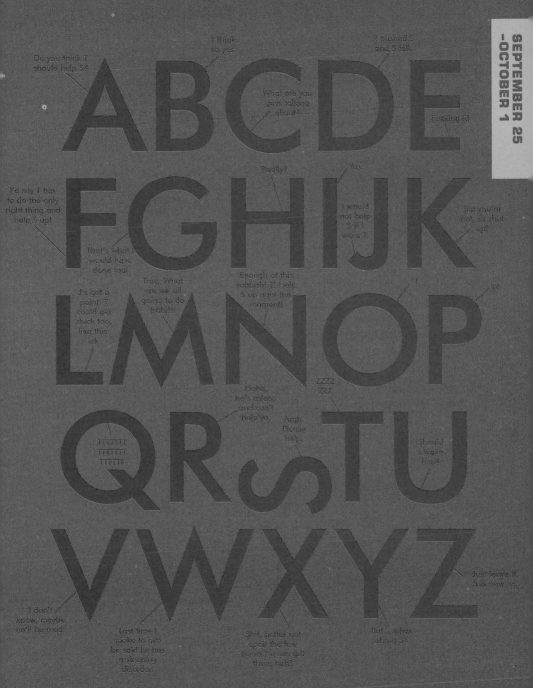

Do you think T should help S?

I think so yes.

? pushed S and S fell.

What are you guys talking about?

Fucking R!

I'd say T has to do the only right thing and help S up!

Really?

Yes...

I would not help S if I were T.

But you're not, so shut up!

That's what I would have done too!

True. What are we all going to do (sob)!!!

Enough of this rubbish! T! Help S up right this moment!

T!

T?

J's got a point. T could get stuck too, like this:

Haha, he's asleep and can't help ya.

ZZZZ ZZZ

Argh. Please help.

Should I wake him?

TTTTTTT TTTTTTT TTTTTT

I don't know, maybe he'll be mad.

Last time I spoke to him he said he has a sleeping disorder.

Shit, better not spoil the few hours he can get then, huh?

Just leave it. S is now :v.

But... what about S?

LEGAL GUIDANCE What to do if they Help: sue them for harassment; what to do if they don't: sue them for negligence.

Monday 25	Tuesday 26	Wednesday 27
9		
10		
11		
12		
13		
14		
15		
16		
17		
18		

Thursday 28	
9	
10	
11	
12	
13	
14	
15	
16	
17	
18	

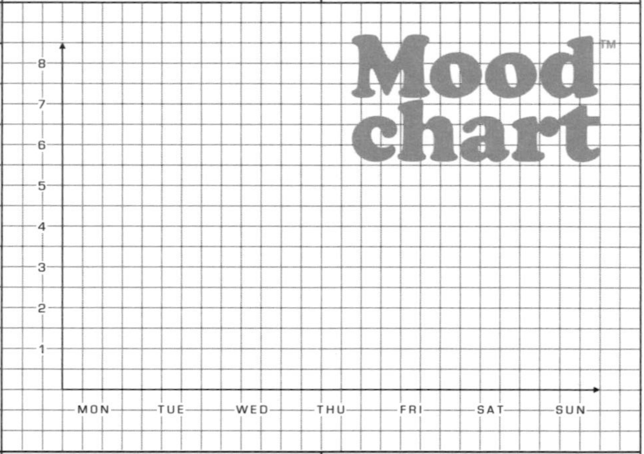

Mood chart™

8
7
6
5
4
3
2
1

MON — TUE — WED — THU — FRI — SAT — SUN

Friday 29	Saturday 30	Sunday 1
9		
10		
11		
12		
13		
14		
15		
16		
17		
18		

Monday 2	Tuesday 3	Wednesday 4
9		
10		
11		
12		
13		
14		
15		
16		
17		
18		

Thursday 5	Friday 6	Saturday 7
9		
10		
11		
12		
13		
14		
15		
16		
17		
18		

Sunday 8
9
10
11
12
13
14
15
16
17
18

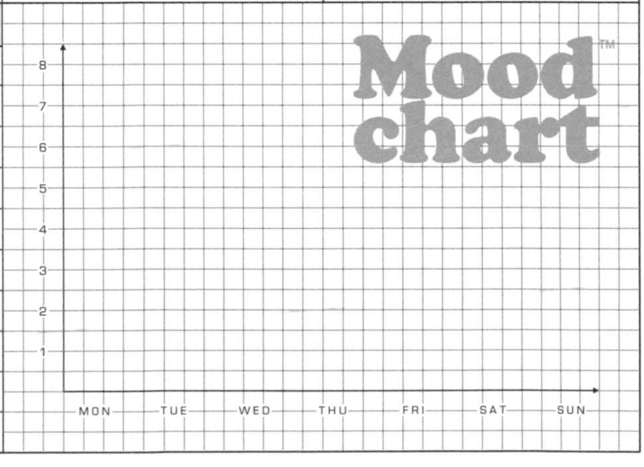

Mood™ chart

8
7
6
5
4
3
2
1

MON — TUE — WED — THU — FRI — SAT — SUN

Open House Week

This week, Benrik followers have full access to each other's houses. Simply register your name and address on www.thiswebsitewillchangeyourlife.com and you will become part of the Benrik Open House network. Starting on Monday at 8 a.m., any Benrikian can visit and stay in <u>any other</u> Benrikian's house, sharing their food and shelter, and their Diary of course. It's like a commune, only without the hippies.

Benrik
User
947 in
reality

Benrik House Rules

Whilst you are a guest of a fellow Benrikian, please observe these simple courtesies.
• No rude comments about decoration
• No thieving of prized possessions
• No dishes left in sink
• No graffiti on the toilet door
• No kicking of owner's cat
• No setting fire to owner's offspring
• No sharing of owner's sexual partner
• No selling house while owner out
• No disrespectful criticism of Benrik
• No hippies

This Week
Insult an alien

All radio waves are beamed up into space at the speed of light, and can travel millions of miles towards faraway galaxies. So, even an amateur CB radio can be used to communicate with other worlds. Today, check it's working by radioing up an appropriate insult. When the alien arrives, tell him or her you were just testing.

Tuesday
Target: Kuiper Belt.
Distance from Earth: 6,000,000,000km.
Likely alien life form: Microbial spores.
Appropriate insult: N/A (non-intelligent life).

Friday
Target: Galaxy M33.
Distance from Earth: 3 million light years.
Likely alien life form: the dinosaurs, who fled the Earth in their spaceship just before the meteorite shower.
Appropriate insult: It's our planet now suckers.

Sunday
Target: Cosmic horizon.
Distance from Earth: 1.3 billion light years.
Likely alien life form: God knows.
Appropriate insult:
Wouldn't risk it on this one.

Monday

Target: Planet Mars.
Distance from Earth: 78,000,000km.
Likely alien life form: Martians.
Appropriate insult: Your mother is
a Venusian whore.

Wednesday

Target: Alpha Centauri.
Distance from Earth:
4.3 light years.
Likely alien life form:
Ozone-breathing octopi.
Appropriate insult: God you're
ugly, even by alien standards.

Thursday

Target: Andromeda.
Distance from Earth: 2.3 million light years.
Likely alien life form: Wise, peace-loving
oil-mining humanoids.
Appropriate insult: Hey hippies, as soon
as we humans master warp drive space
travel technology, you're toast.

Saturday

Target: Zorg Empire.
Distance from Earth: 9.1 million light years.
Likely alien life form: Zorgoids,
three-headed flesh-hungry beasts,
predators of the seven known universes.
Appropriate insult: Come and get some,
you warlike aliens who have mastered warp
drive space travel technology!

The first insult to aliens was the Pioneer plaque, sent out on the unmanned Pioneer 10
spacecraft in March 1972. The plaque is full of symbols meant for extraterrestrial entities, and
thus needs explaining to humans. In the top left, we see two linked circles, which in Zorgon
cosmology are associated with the matter/antimatter split, the root evil of the universe. Below
this, we see the Black Hole of Kloyysnur with the distinctive 14-pronged gravity field responsible
for the galactic holocaust of 549,647,090. To the right, two monstrously deformed creatures,
one of them extending its appendage in the universal sign of "war to extinction". And finally,
the bottom line shows the location of their water-rich planet, a mere 9.1 million light years away.

Monday 9	Tuesday 10	Wednesday 11
9		
10		
11		
12		
13		
14		
15		
16		
17		
18		

Thursday 12

9	
10	
11	
12	
13	
14	
15	
16	
17	
18	

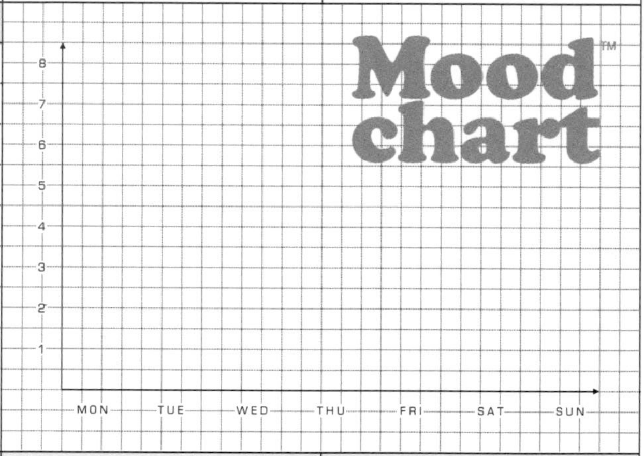

Mood chart™

8
7
6
5
4
3
2
1

MON — TUE — WED — THU — FRI — SAT — SUN

Friday 13	Saturday 14	Sunday 15
9		
10		
11		
12		
13		
14		
15		
16		
17		
18		

Pray to out-of-date gods

Monday 16	Tuesday 17	Wednesday 18
9		
10		
11		
12		
13		
14		
15		
16		
17		
18		

Thursday 19	Friday 20	Saturday 21
9		
10		
11		
12		
13		
14		
15		
16		
17		
18		

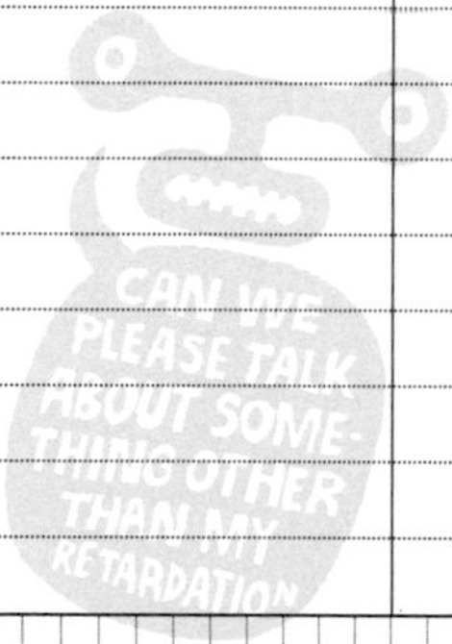

CAN WE PLEASE TALK ABOUT SOMETHING OTHER THAN MY RETARDATION

Sunday 22

9	
10	
11	
12	
13	
14	
15	
16	
17	
18	

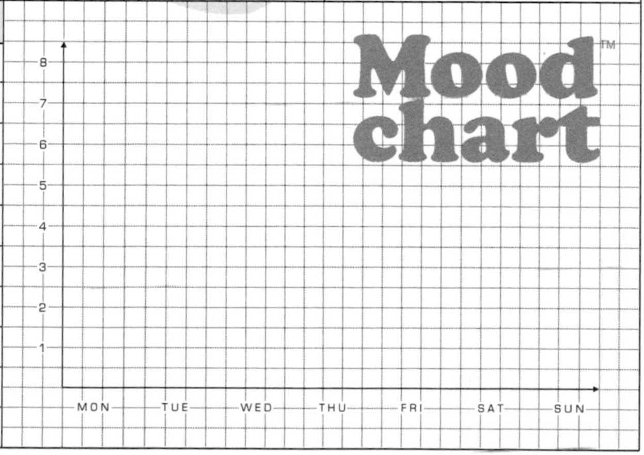

Mood chart™

8
7
6
5
4
3
2
1

MON — TUE — WED — THU — FRI — SAT — SUN

This week, pray to ou

Before the spirit-crushing advent of monotheism, there used to be a much wider variety of gods with extra diligence on behalf of anyone who bothers invoking them. This week, give it a try. W

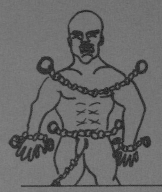

God: Thor
Expertise: Thunder
Background: Protector of all Midgard, wielder of the mighty hammer Mjollnir.
Typical prayer: Dear Thor, pray wield thine mighty hammer Mjollnir tomorrow morning so as to yield rain for my begonias.

God: Minerva
Expertise: Wisdom
Background: Daughter of Jupiter
Typical prayer: Dear Minerva daughter of Jupiter, I am being offered a 3-year fixed rate mortgage with no redemption penalties at 5.15% + £2000 cashback. Tell me what to do.

God: Loki
Expertise: Trouble
Background: Murderer of Balder, the son of Odin and Frigg
Typical prayer: Dear Loki, my neighbour is aggravating me with his loud "metal" music. Please kill him in the night (discreetly).

God: Nerthus
Expertise: Fecundity
Background: Sister and wife of Njörd
Typical prayer: Goddess Nerthus, I have been trying for a baby with my husband for six months now. Before we resort to IVF, would you mind trying to help? We would call the child after you.

God: Mars
Expertise: War, carnage
Background: Earth-god, father of Romulus and Remus
Typical prayer: Dear Mars, would you mind preventing the dissemination of chemical and biological weapons of mass destruction? Spears and arrows were just fine.

God: Ra
Expertise: Sun
Background: Father of Shu and Tefnut
Typical prayer: Dear Ra, we will be holidaying in Malaga from the 13th to the 19th of April. Could you please ensure we enjoy mostly sunshine with little to no cloud cover?

-of-date gods

y now, however, they are extremely bored, and so will act
) knows – if it worked for the Vikings, it could work for you.

God: Poseidon
Expertise: Ocean
Background: Son of Cronus and
Rhea, brother of Zeus
Typical prayer: Dear Poseidon,
please sheathe thy trident until we
dock in Calais as these rough seas
are reversing my digestive process.

God: Thanatos
Expertise: Death
Background: Brother of Hypnos
Typical prayer: Dear Thanatos,
my cousin has cancer of the
thyroid. Leave him alone or I'll
fucking come after you myself.

God: Moloch
Expertise: Infant sacrifice
Background: "Abomination of
the children of Ammon"
Typical prayer: Dear Moloch, my
9-year-old is running wild. I do
not wish to spank him. Could
you please give him a fright of
some kind (apparition, threat of
sacrifice etc.)? Thanks in advance.

God: Gwynn ap Nudd
Expertise: Underworld
Background: Abducted
Creiddylad when she eloped
with Gwythr ap Greidawl
Typical prayer: Dear Gwynn ap
Nudd, I would like to delay my
trip to the Underworld by fifty
years. Could you please make the
necessary arrangements, thanks.

New!

Benrik Gods

The Benrik Gods are the new gods that rule our
lives. Like the ancient Roman household gods,
they govern even the smallest aspects of our
daily existence. But rather than harvests and
crop failure, they deal with fake orgasms and
spam e-mail. Without them, you simply have no
hope of coping with modern life.

Benrik God No 23
Against Corked Wine

Benrik God No 841
Against Split Ends

Benrik God No 88
To Guarantee Orgasm

Benrik God No 5
To Avoid Mobile
Phone Theft

Benrik God No 155
For Prompt Pizza
Delivery

Benrik God No 89
To Ward Off Partner
Snoring

Benrik God No 809
Against Overeating
Raspberries

Benrik God No 10
To Ward Off Spam
Email

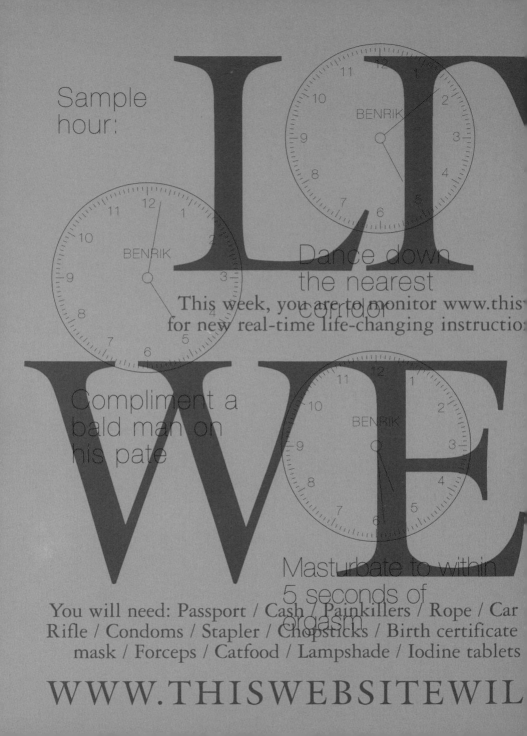

Sample
hour:

LI

This week, you are to monitor www.this
for new real-time life-changing instructio

Dance down
the nearest
corridor

WE

Compliment a
bald man on
his pate

Masturbate to within
5 seconds of
orgasm

You will need: Passport / Cash / Painkillers / Rope / Car
Rifle / Condoms / Stapler / Chopsticks / Birth certificate
mask / Forceps / Catfood / Lampshade / Iodine tablets

WWW.THISWEBSITEWIL

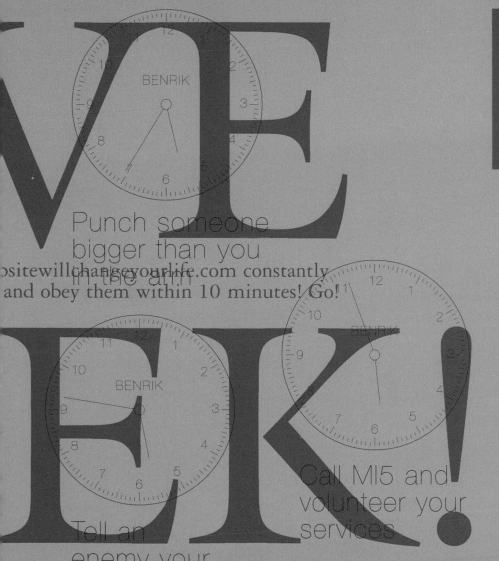

VE
EK!

Punch someone
bigger than you
in the arm.

ositewillchangeyourlife.com constantly
and obey them within 10 minutes! Go!

Call MI5 and
volunteer your
services

Tell an
enemy your
middle name

changes of clothes / Sleeping pills / Prozac / First-aid kit /
pstick / Jumpsuit / Post-its / Waterproof camera / Oxygen
iolin / Sleeping bag / Telescope / Machete / Toothpaste.

CHANGEYOURLIFE.COM

Monday 23	Tuesday 24	Wednesday 25
9		
10		
11		
12		
13		
14		
15		
16		
17		
18		

Thursday 26	
9	
10	
11	
12	
13	
14	
15	
16	
17	
18	

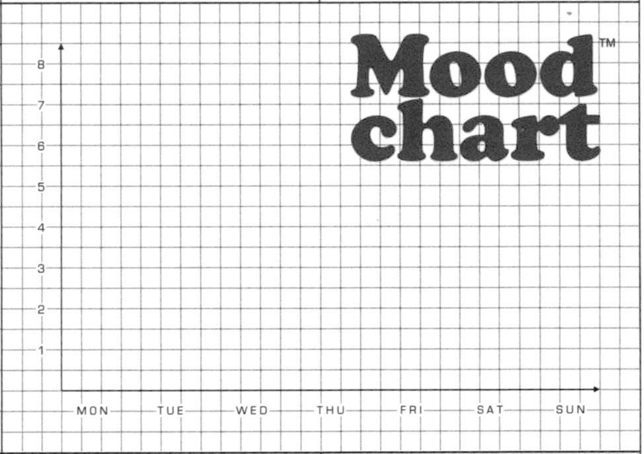

8
7
6
5
4
3
2
1

MON — TUE — WED — THU — FRI — SAT — SUN

Mood chart ™

Friday 27	Saturday 28	Sunday 29
9		
10		
11		
12		
13		
14		
15		
16		
17		
18		

I'VE HAD ENOUGH! FROM NOW ON LET US ALL LIVE IN A FREE WORLD!

Animal Week: view everyone and everything sexually

Monday 30	Tuesday 31	Wednesday 1
9		
10		
11		
12		
13		
14		
15		
16		
17		
18		

Thursday 2	Friday 3	Saturday 4
9		
10		
11		
12		
13		
14		
15		
16		
17		
18		

Sunday 5
9
10
11
12
13
14
15
16
17
18

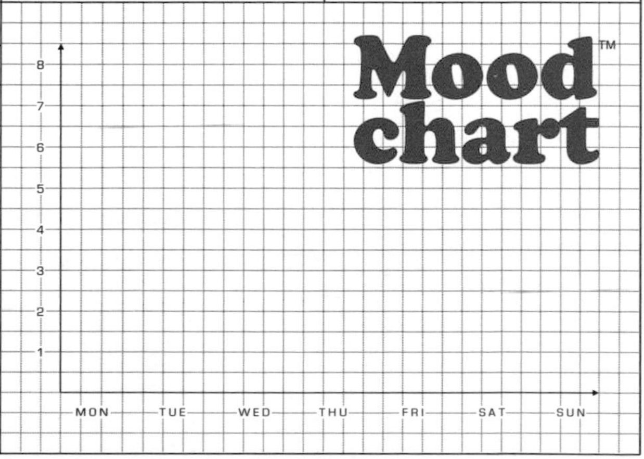

Mood chart ™

8
7
6
5
4
3
2
1

MON — TUE — WED — THU — FRI — SAT — SUN

Animal week:
view everyone &
everything sexually

Ditch civilization and its superfluous
airs and graces, and return to your
primeval animal roots: your sole
Darwinian purpose in life is to
procreate. This week, everyone is to
mate each other indiscriminately in the
manner of Viagra-abusing chimps.

Present your
posterior to/bum to
passing alpha males

Smell passing
strangers

Piss on the ground to
mark your territory

Stare at people's
crotches

Greet everyone
with a low guttural
moan

Groar

Brush up against
people you fancy

Bite, maim or kill your
sexual competitors

View anyone bending
over as an invitation to
immediate intercourse

Ding
Ding

Promiscuity Chart (tick every mating)

	1	2	3	4	5	6	7	8	9	10
Monday										
Tuesday										
Wednesday										
Thursday										
Friday										
Saturday										
Sunday										

Benrik
Animal
Week!

Benrik
Collector
Task

This week, make a shrine about someone you don't know but see on a regular basis, then show it to them.

80 - 82

John's morning routine

The insurance house.

Getting off the bus.

<u>Where John lives:</u> No12 Hickory Lane
<u>About his home:</u> John lives in a <u>nice house</u> with a garden. The garden <u>has a gate</u> with an old padlock. The house has <u>nice</u> curtains. The living room has a TV <u>wich is often on</u> in the evening, sometimes even past <u>midnight.</u> John lives in the same house as a <u>woman.</u> She looks like a WITCH. She <u>wants to hurt</u> John, but I <u>won't</u> let her haha. ~~Then~~ John gets a <u>lot of mail.</u> Here is a <u>postcard</u> from his <u>mum</u> in New Zeeland (Susan):

Welcome To New Zealand

Lovely summer.

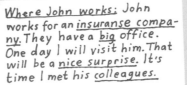

Make a shrine about someone you don't know

Monday 6	Tuesday 7	Wednesday 8
9		
10		
11		
12		
13		
14		
15		
16		
17		
18		

Thursday 9		
9		
10		
11		
12		
13		
14		
15		
16		
17		
18		

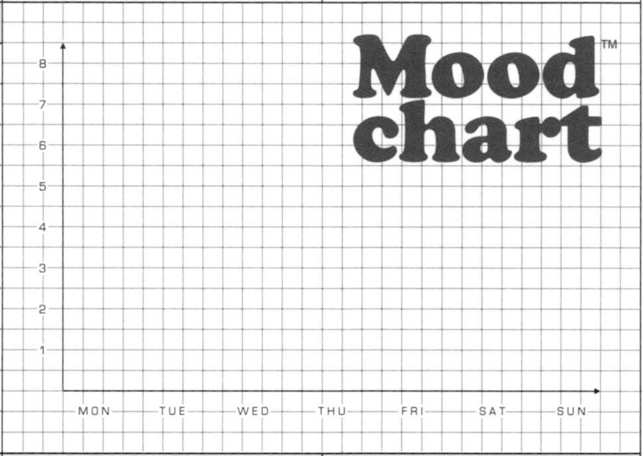

Mood chart™

8
7
6
5
4
3
2
1

MON — TUE — WED — THU — FRI — SAT — SUN

Friday 10	Saturday 11	Sunday 12
9		
10		
11		
12		
13		
14		
15		
16		
17		
18		

Monday 13	Tuesday 14	Wednesday 15
9		
10		
11		
12		
13		
14		
15		
16		
17		
18		

Thursday 16	Friday 17	Saturday 18
9		
10		
11		
12		
13		
14		
15		
16		
17		
18		

Sunday 19
9
10
11
12
13
14
15
16
17
18

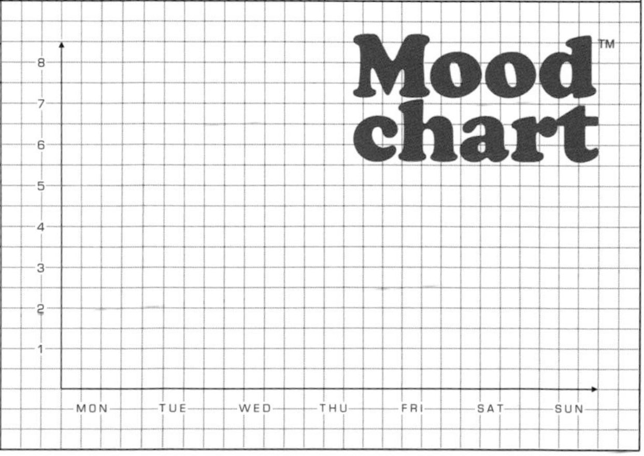

Apply for a job that you think is beneath you

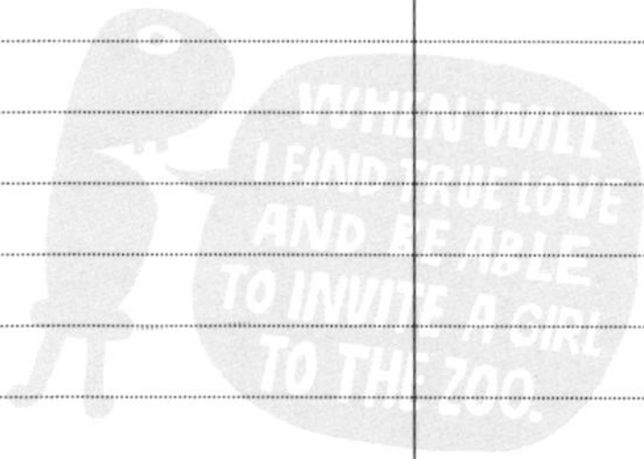

Mood chart™

8
7
6
5
4
3
2
1

MON TUE WED THU FRI SAT SUN

Bargain Prostitute.

The guy who sandpapers the pieces of glass that washes up on our beaches.

Part-time Horse-shit-Eater.

Pilgrim without a goal.

Under-paid leaf-counter.

Acidic substances Taster.

King without a castle.

Lassie's fluffer.

Party-police.

Corked-Wine Taster.

Karaoke-singer of Celine Dion.

Executioner of cute animals.

Messenger
of bad news.

This week, apply for a job that you think is beneath you

Could you really be a fast food employee, a checkout guy, or a rubbish collector for the council? We assume that these so-called "menial" occupations are within anyone's reach, but perhaps you simply don't have what it takes. Apply and find out this week, and get a better picture of your limits in the process.

Kiwi-shaver.

Programmer
of Sinclair
computers.

C-list
Paparazzi.

Soon-to-retire
Arena-Sweeper.

Unexploded-
mines
polisher.

Lawyer
for the
long-term
unemployed.

Piranha-
bait.

HELLO

Call any family members over 70 first; the older and more experienced, the better. If you have none, email one of these retirement homes and respectfully ask that they forward your question to a senior citizen.

Business decisions
Mount Olivet Nursing Home, Devon
(mountolivet@grayareas.co.uk)

Romantic decisions
All Hallows, Suffolk
(admin@allhallowsnursinghome.org.uk)

Political decisions
Kestrel Grove, Hertfordshire
(home@kestrelgrove.co.uk)

Medical decisions
Buxton Lodge Nursing Home, Surrey
(care@buxtonlodge.co.uk)

Artistic decisions
Chilton House, Buckinghamshire
(enquires@chiltonhouse.co.uk)

Legal decisions
Aronal Cottage Rest & Nursing Home, West Sussex
(info@aronalcottage.co.uk)

Military decisions
Taymer Nursing Home, Bedfordshire
(matron@taymer.co.uk)

Scientific decisions
Villa Maria, Melbourne, Australia
(villamaria@villamaria.com.au)

Cultural decisions
Haresbrook Care Centre, Worcestershire
(care.haresbrook@virgin.net)

This week, obey your elders and betters

Most human societies cherish and respect the wisdom of their oldest members; the elders are chiefs, leaders, high priests. Western society, however, consigns them to quiet retirement homes and social irrelevance. Reverse this sad state of affairs this week: let none of us make a single decision without consulting someone over the age of 70.

Obey your elders and betters

Monday 20	Tuesday 21	Wednesday 22
9		
10		
11		
12		
13		
14		
15		
16		
17		
18		

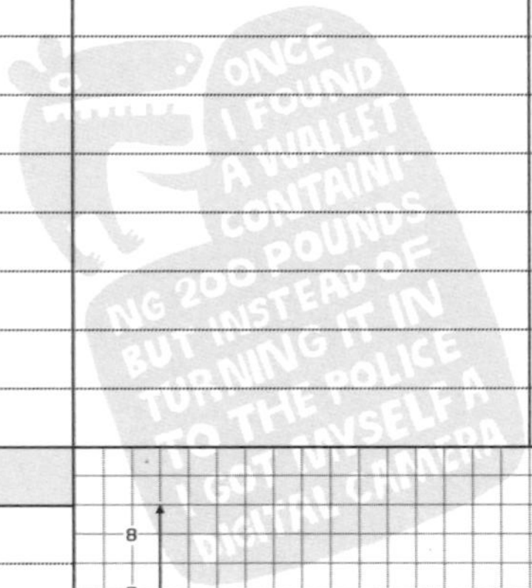

Thursday 23		
9		
10		
11		
12		
13		
14		
15		
16		
17		
18		

Mood chart™

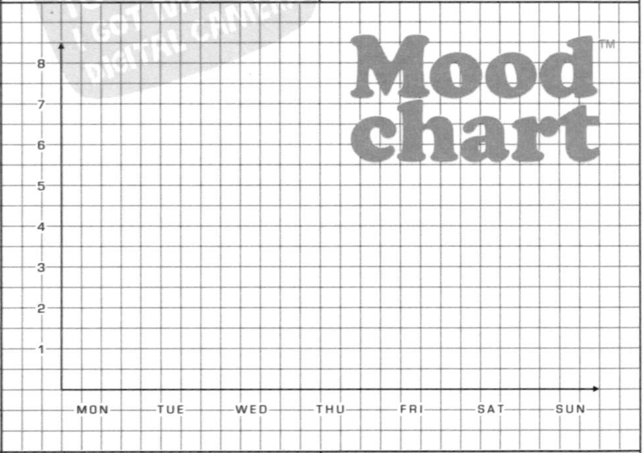

MON—TUE—WED—THU—FRI—SAT—SUN

Friday 24	Saturday 25	Sunday 26
9		
10		
11		
12		
13		
14		
15		
16		
17		
18		

Monday 27	Tuesday 28	Wednesday 29
9		
10		
11		
12		
13		
14		
15		
16		
17		
18		

Thursday 30	Friday 1	Saturday 2
9		
10		
11		
12		
13		
14		
15		
16		
17		
18		

Sunday 3	
9	
10	
11	
12	
13	
14	
15	
16	
17	
18	

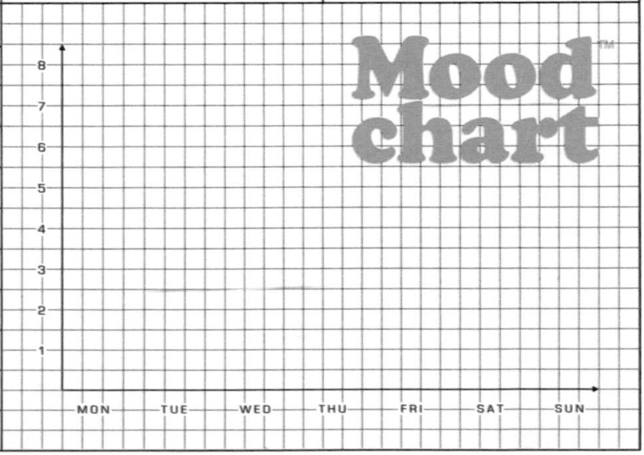

Go dogging as a Jehovah's witness

Mood chart ™

8
7
6
5
4
3
2
1

MON — TUE — WED — THU — FRI — SAT — SUN

This week, go dogging as a Jehovah's Witness

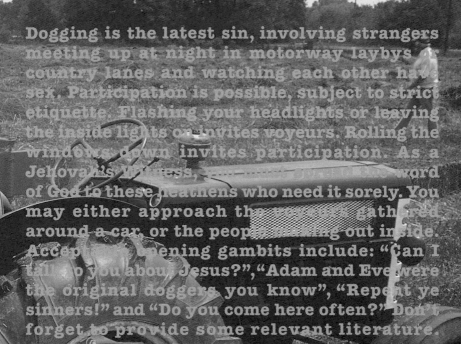

Dogging is the latest sin, involving strangers meeting up at night in motorway laybys or country lanes and watching each other have sex. Participation is possible, subject to strict etiquette. Flashing your headlights or leaving the inside lights on invites voyeurs. Rolling the windows down invites participation. As a Jehovah's Witness, you must spread the word of God to these heathens who need it sorely. You may either approach the voyeurs gathered around a car, or the people making out inside. Acceptable opening gambits include: "Can I talk to you about Jesus?", "Adam and Eve were the original doggers, you know", "Repent ye sinners!" and "Do you come here often?" Don't forget to provide some relevant literature.

Mummy's milk tastes
rather sour these days,
don't you think?

That's because
she's on lithium.

Baby Talk Week

This week, communicate only as a baby would. You may squeal, giggle, produce wordless noise or cry. If someone breastfeeds you, you've succeeded.

Lexicon

Goo!	Yes, that pleases me
Grr!	No, that is not to my liking
Goo grrr!	I am in two minds on this one
Areuh!	Life is good
Euhhhh!	Life is so-so
Wahhhh!	Life is bad
WAaaaaH!!	Life is unfair
WAAHH!!!	I didn't fucking ask to be born
Ahaaaaagh!!	I demand attention
Burp!	That meal was delicious
His!	I will now regurgitate it
Heehee!	I am laughing at you not with you
Mama!	Mother
Dada!	I assume you're my father
Gaga!	Who the hell are you?
Poopoo!	Oh shit
Eeeeeeyeh!!	Eeeeeeyeh!
Mrfittplbtrch!	I need urgent medical attention

Baby Talk Week

Monday 4	Tuesday 5	Wednesday 6
9		
10		
11		
12		
13		
14		
15		
16		
17		
18		

Thursday 7	
9	8
10	7
11	6
12	5
13	4
14	3
15	2
16	1
17	
18	MON — TUE — WED — THU — FRI — SAT — SUN

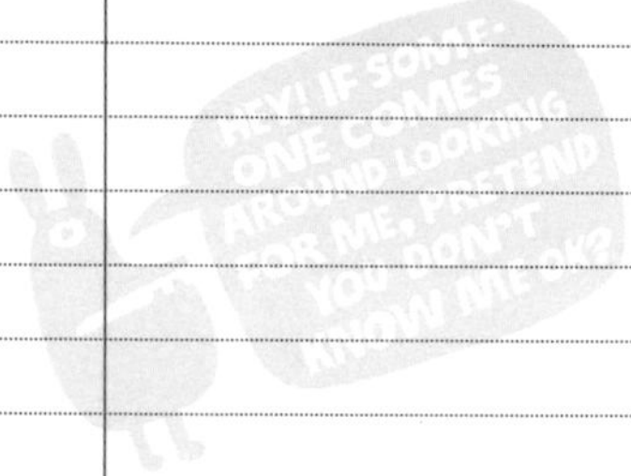

Mood chart™

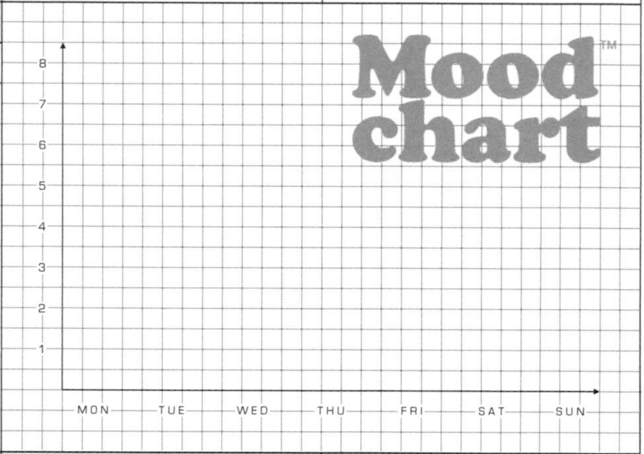

Friday 8	Saturday 9	Sunday 10
9		
10		
11		
12		
13		
14		
15		
16		
17		
18		

Monday 11	Tuesday 12	Wednesday 13
9		
10		
11		
12		
13		
14		
15		
16		
17		
18		

Thursday 14	Friday 15	Saturday 16
9		
10		
11		
12		
13		
14		
15		
16		
17		
18		

Sunday 17
9
10
11
12
13
14
15
16
17
18

Mood chart™

8
7
6
5
4
3
2
1

MON — TUE — WED — THU — FRI — SAT — SUN

This week, volunteer fo

Drugs companies need to test their new prod
cash by participating in their trials. But it's no
opportunity for radical life change. These are
before research has sanitized them. Pick a cu
cutting-edge side effects: night vision, telepa
of how that would pep up your daily routine! C

Worst-case scenario:
you'll be able to bring an expensive lawsuit!

A strain of
human DNA

Where do I sign up?

Not so fast! To qualify for most clinical trials, you should be a healthy male aged 18–45. Women aged 18–65 may apply but usually need to be post-menopausal or infertile, as the danger to any fetus from these trials is too great. However, if you are very keen, ask if you may sign a legal waiver. You will need to undergo a medical check-up to ascertain your suitability. You will usually be asked to stay overnight, and will be expected to attend daytime clinics for blood tests and other forms of monitoring. Important: Make sure to ask for early Phase I trials, or even volunteer for late-phase animal trials if you want to guarantee noticeably life-changing results. Our tip: invasive trials pay better.

a medical experiment

ts on human volunteers. You can earn decent
about the money, it's about the unrivalled
ugs in the early stages of development,
:ing-edge drug, and chances are you'll develop
y or radioactive superpowers perhaps. Think
II today and volunteer your services.

Case studies

(these examples starting this week are fully-booked, but others like them are available)

Start date	Monday 11/12/06	Monday 11/12/06	Monday 11/12/06	Tuesday 12/12/06	Friday 15/12/06	Friday 15/12/06	Sunday 17/12/06
Study code	JS0098X	Sanuspol 3000z	Phfx/788/f act.4	TT-x545	RD2100000 M7	DRF003/ 2a	Ch56/ 44−0004
Study type	New laxative drug	Kidney cleansing agent	Cancer vaccine	Drug side-effects on spinal fluid	Skin reaction to GM bio-enzyme YK9	Blood recoagulant	Potential vaccine for Marburg haemorrhagic fever
Country	UK	UK	Belgium	UK	USA	Andorra	Tasmania
Overnight stays	1	1	4	5	7	1 to 14+ (depending response)	59
Daily visits	Medical x2 morning visits	Medical	Medical x3, annual check-up (indef.)	Medical x2, annual check-up for 6 years	Medical x2, 12 monthly visits	Medical x3	Medical, 2 month stay
Risk factor	6/10	2/10	7/10	8/10	8/10	8/10	9/10
Payment	£1,450	£190 + travel expenses	£2,500	£4,125	$2,200	£1500 min	£6,980 + airfare

This week, ruin Christmas's repu

·Monday:
Stash a bottle of
Jim Beam under
your beard and take
conspicuous swigs.

·Wednesday:
Read children's letters
to Santa in public,
tearing them into little
pieces with a ho-ho-ho.

·Friday:
Set up a street
stand selling
reindeer burgers.

·Tuesday:
Visit Harrods
and shoplift toys
into your sack.

·Thursday:
Accost shoppers and
confess that Christmas
is just a commercial
rip-off these days.

·Saturday:
As small kids sit
on your knee, whisper
to them that Xmas is
cancelled.

·Sunday:
Pull off legitimate Santa
Clauses' beards whilst shouting
"You fucking impostor!"

Ruin Father Christmas's reputation

Monday 18	Tuesday 19	Wednesday 20
9		
10		
11		
12		
13		
14		
15		
16		
17		
18		

Thursday 21	
9	
10	
11	
12	
13	
14	
15	
16	
17	
18	

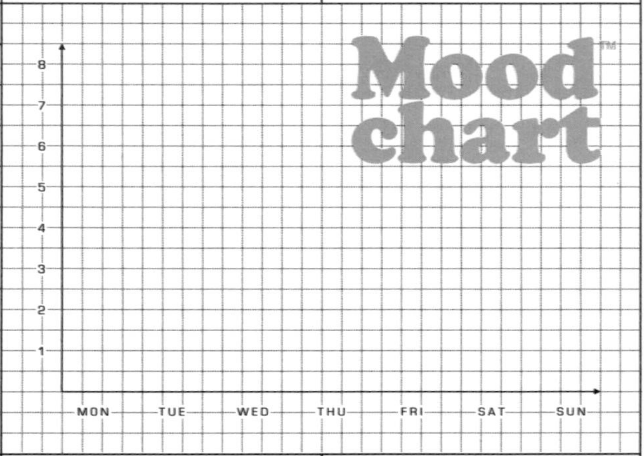

Mood chart™

8
7
6
5
4
3
2
1

MON — TUE — WED — THU — FRI — SAT — SUN

Friday 22	Saturday 23	Sunday 24
9		
10		
11		
12		
13		
14		
15		
16		
17		
18		

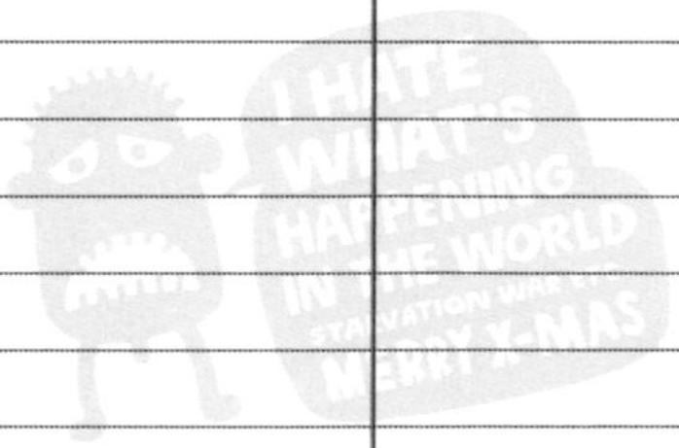

I HATE WHAT'S HAPPENING IN THE WORLD STARVATION MERRY X-MAS

Monday 25 CHRISTMAS DAY	Tuesday 26 BOXING DAY	Wednesday 27
9		
10		
11		
12		
13		
14		
15		
16		
17		
18		

Thursday 28	Friday 29	Saturday 30
9		
10		
11		
12		
13		
14		
15		
16		
17		
18		

Sunday 31 NEW YEAR'S DAY
9
10
11
12
13
14
15
16
17
18

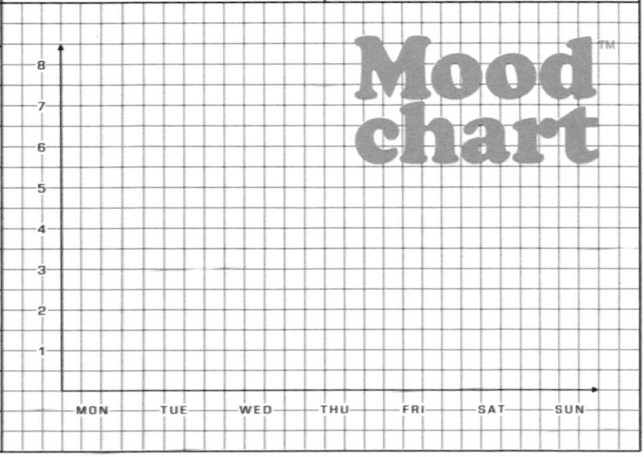

Gamble everything you have

Mood chart™

8
7
6
5
4
3
2
1

MON — TUE — WED — THU — FRI — SAT — SUN

ALL OR NOTHING WEEK: THIS WEEK GAMBLE EVERYTHING YOU HAVE

DON'T LET THE AMERICAN DREAM SLIP AWAY! THIS WEEK, SELL YOUR HOUSE, PAWN THE TV, MAX OUT YOUR CREDIT CARDS – AND ROLL THE DICE ON YOUR CASH!

Ten
commandments
of casino
gambling

1 - Thou shalt expect to lose.

2 - Thou shalt trust the odds, not hunches.

3 - Thou shalt not over-bet thy bankroll.

4 - Thou shalt not believe in betting systems.

5 - Thou shalt not hedge thy bets.

6 - Thou shalt covet good rules.

7 - Thou shalt not make side bets.

8 - Thou shalt have good gambling etiquette.

9 - Thou shalt honor thy gambling debts.

10 - Thou shalt tip.

**NO RISK,
NO REWARD...**

Self-Assessment

How well are you doing? Keep track of these key indicators
week after week to help measure your life-change.

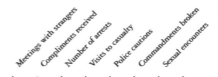

	Meetings with strangers	Compliments received	Number of arrests	Visits to casualty	Police cautions	Commandments broken	Sexual encounters	
Week 1: Warm-up Week								
Week 2: Be a pathological liar								
Week 3: Mini-prostitution Week								
Week 4: Prepare for Chinese World Domination								
Week 5: Cause an international security alert								
Week 6: Claim you're from the future								
Week 7: Valentine Week: Attract Your Opposite								
Week 8: Slavery Week								
Week 9: Commit all Seven Sins								
Week 10: Help fix the charts								
Week 11: Mouth obscenities to passing strangers								
Week 12: Pretend you're a doctor								
Week 13: Run for US president								
Week 14: Step on as many people's feet as possible								
Week 15: Ask a billionaire for money								
Week 16: Imaginary Friend Week								
Week 17: Buddhist Fundamentalism Week								
Week 18: Rebel against your astrological sign								
Week 19: Fake your own kidnapping								
Week 20: Aversion Diet Week								
Week 21: Play God with other peoples' lives								
Week 22: Lend your mobile to a homeless person								
Week 23: Put yourself up for sale on eBay								
Week 24: Have a row with everyone you meet								
Week 25: Try out all major religions								
Week 26: Act like you're invisible								
Week 27: Insure your best feature								
Week 28: Cause a diplomatic incident								
Week 29: Make your dreams come true								
Week 30: Stalk writers to become their muse								
Week 31: Freak Tan Week								
Week 32: Run away as far as you can								
Week 33: Spark a political debate								
Week 34: Add your touch to an artistic masterpiece								
Week 35: Marry a Benrik mail-order spouse								
Week 36: Assess people's potential for evil and act in consequence								
Week 37: Plagiarism Week								
Week 38: Live like you're in a commercial								
Week 39: Test the Nation								
Week 40: Open House Week								
Week 41: Insult an alien								
Week 42: Pray to out-of-date gods								
Week 43: Live Week								
Week 44: Animal Week: view everyone and everything sexually								
Week 45: Make a shrine about someone you don't know								
Week 46: Apply for a job that you think is beneath you								
Week 47: Obey your elders and betters								
Week 48: Go dogging as a Jehovah's witness								
Week 49: Baby Talk Week								
Week 50: Volunteer for a medical experiment								
Week 51: Ruin Father Christmas's reputation								
Week 52: Gamble everything you have								
Total:								

New friends	New enemies	Near death experiences	Spiritual rebirths	Pay rises	Body count	Spontaneous hugs received	Kilos lost	New tattoos	New scars	Newspaper mentions	Lawsuits won	Lawsuits lost	Lawsuits settled	Food poisoning incidents	Insults received	Psychiatric evaluations	Coups d'état witnessed	Coups d'état caused

Life-Change Checklist

If you have followed the Diary from its first modern edition in 2004,
this is what you should have achieved by now. Tick each task to confirm
you have performed it, then go back and do those you've missed.

Start smoking □ Write the opening sentence of your début novel □ Stick an "out of order" sign on public infrastructure □ Gaze at everyone as if they were the love of your life □ Throw something away that you like □ Work out your life's travel plans and book them □ Masturbate to Benrik's fantasies □ Do something before breakfast □ Meet Jonas Jansson □ Introduce yourself to someone you never speak to □ Send a letter to a mass murderer □ Flatter people to see if it does get you anywhere □ Be gay for a day □ Discreetly give the finger to everyone □ Eat nothing but asparagus □ Kill something □ Pretend to be a secret agent □ Help create the world's longest poem □ Feel patriotic about a country of your choice □ Agree to meet someone in ten years' time □ Get a quote from a plastic surgeon □ Barter □ List the things you will never do before you die □ Choose what you'd like to be reincarnated as □ Choose your final meal on death row and make it □ Dial a phone number at random and read this message from David Koresh □ Celebrate Nauru National Day □ Control your dreams □ Look out for the paranormal □ Write to a dictator to stop torture □ Give little tasks to people around you □ Say nothing all day □ Do a runner □ Spend time in church □ Learn Swedish □ Play a practical joke □ Apply for a knighthood □ Walk barefoot on grass □ Defy superstition □ Come up with a romantic compliment that has never been made before □ Ask a stranger what first impression you make □ Make a citizen's arrest □ Make people notice you □ Be blind □ Return all your junk mail □ Live the Heavy Metal lifestyle at its most decadent □ Try food that scares you □ Decide what skills to pass on in your family □ Lift an object with your mind □ Find out how symmetrical you are □ Prepare pagan circles wherever you go □ Break a world record □ Send a letter to someone at random with a photo of yourself, a £5 note, no explanation and no sender address and see what comes of it □ Learn a poem by heart □ Go without water □ Choose one hair on your body that you will let grow 1m long □ Fire someone from your entourage □ Find out if you are a psychopath □ Get sued □ Call your kindergarten and ask them if they've found your rattle □ Get a hobby □ Express your views □ Visit Gino's in Louisiana □ Wear shoes that are one size too small □ Design your own logo □ Make sure your circle of friends is politically correct □ Eat a piece of furniture □ Lure a fly onto this page and swat it □ Throw away an apple core in a park □ Go to the wrong side of the tracks □ Send a message in morse and see if anyone responds □ Measure your biceps □ Primal-scream □ Help collapse a currency □ Invent a new way of peeling potatoes □ Write your will □ Show some cosmic humility □ Avoid all sources of electromagnetic energy □ Learn how to spot the aliens among us □ Stockpile free sugar □ Rap □ Send Benrik one pound for every swear word that escapes your lips □ Experience the Lord's plight with Benrik's DIY crucifixion kit □ Become a chocolate junkie □ Break the Ten Commandments □ Cleanse your bowels □ Lie to someone about your age □ Treat your partner mean, keep'em keen □ Tattoo a banana □ See a film beginning in F □ Tattoo a banana □ Violate a law of your choice □ Go deaf □ Spend no money all day □ Learn an emergency first aid procedure □ Train a parrot to say unpalatable truths □ Count your blessings □ Write a letter to your local newspaper to achieve a high profile in your community □ Defy hierarchy □ Invent a new colour □ Hack into a computer network □ Make sure your parents know you love them □ Find out if cheese does give you nightmares □ Bleed here for DNA purposes □ Jam the KKK phone line □ Build a nest and see if a bird comes □ Distribute friendship coupons □ Start an urban myth □ Prepare your last words ahead of time □ Change someone's mind □ Leave a note on someone's car windshield □ Help resolve an intractable global geopolitical crisis □ Spend a day underwater □ Write a message to the future □ Talk to a plant □ Confess to a priest □ Redesign an everyday product □ Behave as if you were playing chess □ Find a way of making £10 grow into £100 in one day □ Compose a poem and leave it in a public place to brighten up someone's day □ Make prolonged eye contact with everyone you meet □ Shoplift □ Share someone's pain □ Develop your very own eccentricity □ Voodoo an enemy □ Speak only in clichés □ Sell something you've made □ Stick a message on a fruit □ Tend to your body hair □ Go on strike □ Put a lost dog ad up and see whether one turns up □ Try seducing someone out of your league □ Go through a phase □ Pretend to be a tourist □ Write to your local authority asking that your street be renamed after you □ Return to childhood □ Write down your everyday conversation □ Join a political party □ Become as clean as the day you were born □ Bury a treasure □ Explore your deeper feelings towards a family member □ Improve your signature □ Have a good cry □ Send a message in a bottle □ Test yourself for pregnancy □ Be entirely serious □ Have a row in public □ Sunbathe topless □ Take a lover □ Protest violently against the government □ Write down your dreams □ Stage a crime in front of a CCTV camera and see if anyone comes to the rescue □ Measure your IQ □ Go to your nearest maternity ward and welcome a new life □ Start a collection □ Volume-test your neighbours □ Live this day as if it were your last □ Find a way of including the word "Vortex" in all your conversations □ Jump a queue □ Go without electricity □ Do something radical with your hair □ Go to a supermarket and enter all the competitions □ Have your head examined □ Deny yourself something □ Buy a newspaper and read only the ads □ Test the butterfly effect □ Experience a new emotion □ Send a telegram □ Bullshit □ Do everything backwards □ Make sure your name is on the internet □ Use your left hand all day □ Extend your lifespan □ Expand your vocabulary □ Eat everything using chopsticks □ Do everything society urges you to do □ Twin yourself with a foreigner □ Read your own palm □ Picture everyone naked □ Invent a new punctuation mark □ Test God's existence □ Destroy photos that make you look ugly □ Throw a sickie □ Send Benrik money □ Do something to make it to the top □ Give someone a totally impractical gift □ Put a personal ad in the paper □ Test your memory □ Dispose of a potential weapon □ Trace your High School sweetheart and offer to meet up □ Discover a star □ Talk to a child □ Abstain from any sexual contact □ Find your namesake □ Go to the zoo and do feed the animals □ Trust someone with your life □ Do a good deed □ Bodybuild a single muscle □ Make sure the police are acting within the law □ Ignore the media □ Monitor your sexual thoughts □ Write down and acknowledge your biggest mistake in life □ Start a fight □ Propose to a complete stranger □ Find out if you were adopted □ Say hello to everyone in the street □ Be the last man standing □ Invent your very own milkshake □ Report a UFO sighting □ Draw attention to an unsung hero □ Perform a self-medical □ Act like you're worth millions □ Place flowers on an old unattended gravestone □ Take one memorable photo □ Count the 2000 commercial messages you are exposed to per day □ Check how good your doctor is □ Sample as many of the finest things in life as your circumstances allow □ Do without underwear □ Give humanity something to remember you by □ Bail a stranger out of jail □ Take a cold shower □ Learn a ballet step □ Embrace Mother Earth □ Choose your motto and live by it □ Kiss someone where they've never been kissed before □ Hitchhike □

Date yourself □ Send some roses to your long-suffering mother □ Become a master of wine □ Disappear □ Sign-up to go into space □ Dig at the end of a rainbow □ Eat nothing but red meat □ Do something kinky □ Convince a kid Santa does exist □ Swap jobs with a friend □ Collect your belly button fluff and send it in □ Make a speech □ Join the freemasons □ Pay for sex □ Celebrate life by drinking nothing but champagne □ Challenge everyone you meet to a game of noughts and crosses □ Sketch someone opposite you on public transport and see how they react □ Catch Father Christmas □ Disinherit a relative □ Increase your tolerance to hot food □ Claim you're Jesus □ Promote the Diary □ Eat part of a loved one □ Marry Jonas Jansson □ Emigrate to New Zealand □ Write a bestseller □ Buy a stranger flowers □ Boycott something that's never been boycotted □ Apply to an orgy □ Dump your partner □ Test a proverb □ Review this Diary □ Free someone today! □ Test the power of prayer □ Feast all weekend □ Invent your own traffic rule and obey it □ Single out one of your toes for special treatment □ Record the next generation of canned laughter □ Speak to people as if you were a global corporation □ Find your self □ Live at night □ Download and spread a computer virus □ Speak only Esperanto □ Learn to hypnotize yourself □ Count down to everything □ Threaten a foreign country □ Publicly humiliate yourself □ Argue people out of their purchases □ Disagree with everything □ Borrow a lock of pubic hair from your neighbour □ Break gym etiquette □ Find Lord Lucan □ Send a Valentine to someone unloved □ Get psychoanalysed by Benrik □ Eat this book □ Enforce the "customer is always right" rule □ Act schizophrenic □ Get rained on □ Find out your position in the line of succession to the throne □ Denounce someone to the government □ Redistribute wealth □ Hand deliver your emails □ Fake amnesia □ Gatecrash a funeral □ Rage against the machine □ Paint a self-portrait □ Wreak havoc on a microscopic scale □ Mother your mother □ Do whatever others tell you to do □ Release a dove for peace □ Recover a childhood memory □ Dig for oil □ Bend your gender □ Use graphology to manipulate others □ Apply to Madame Tussaud's □ Get back at someone □ Make a baby □ Act like a teenager □ Join the Benrik T-shirt Club □ Sing Wagner in the shower □ Give Ada Peach her 15 minutes of fame □ Claim to have been abducted by aliens □ Fast all weekend □ Drive the Devil out of a loved one □ Visit a complete stranger in hospital □ Become a hermit □ Act hyperactive □ Help destroy an ugly building □ Praise an unsung achievement □ Start a relationship with a fellow Diarist □ Commit treason □ Stalk an animal □ Act suspiciously □ Spaz! □ Insist on speaking to the media □ Tip abnormally □ Make a pilgrimage □ Pour cocaine down an anthill □ Go naturist □ Sign a petition against everything □ Enter a trailer trash competition □ Put yourself forward for cloning □ Deface a powerful image □ Visit Benrikland □ Pack a lunch for a homeless person □ Be a good spouse □ Practise your hunter-gatherer skills □ Become a movie extra □ Watch the sun set □ Win $$$ if you recognize your DNA sequence! □ Impress your librarian □ Mess up your kids so they turn into Picasso □ Plant marijuana outside a government building □ Be a virtual exhibitionist □ Self-medicate □ Foment revolution □ Confuse future archaeologists □ Hit someone with a frying pan □ Spend exactly £37 □ Hold hands all day □ Carry your own muzak □ Post your dirty pics on the net □ Welcome all passing strangers into your home □ Work out what your dreams are telling you to do and do it □ Send a drink over to someone □ Listen to a loved one's inner workings □ Prepare for Judgement Day □ Rearrange your local supermarket □ Make people believe you're a cyborg □ Sing everything □ Let the colour orange dictate your life □ Jump to cause an earthquake □ Leave a trail behind you, Hansel&Gretel style □ Help a student cheat □ Become a superhero □ Write and thank your most influential teacher □ Assess your father's performance so far □ Bite animals back □ Choose a tattoo for someone □ Climb your way down the corporate pyramid □ Use your remote control for evil purposes □ Stroke a bus or train conductor as payment for the fare □ Make your special imprint on sporting history □ Hijack a public performance □ Presell your memoirs □ Have all your food tasted for poison □ Spend the weekend up a tree □ Help reconquer America □ Write a letter to your future self □ Speak the unspeakable □ Sell your sperm or eggs □ Impulse-buy □ Invoke an evil spirit □ Stare into people's homes □ Speedread *War & Peace* □ Do everything in slow motion □ Attempt to be noticed from space □ Dumb down □ Mislead a tourist □ Take part in the great cycle of life □ Look out for subtle body language □ Fight for your country! □ Appear on TV □ Ask everyone you meet to jump □ Grimace as the wind changes □ Internet Vigilante Day □ Try Prozac and increase your level of happiness □ Kidnap a worm □ Stare at a single work of art for hours □ Live the life of a 13th century peasant □ Try self-acupuncture □ Carry a hidden weapon □ Serenade someone □ Have a sleep somewhere random □ Draw God □ Send your suggestions to the government □ Price tag all your possessions □ Make someone hate you □ Write a message on a banknote □ Let a dog walk you □ Discover who you were in a past life □ Practise extreme fruitarianism □ Fire your bank for the sake of it □ Let children rule the world □ Make sure your body survives you □ Topple a dictator using the internet □ Go back to school □ Make an insect's day □ Change the weather □ Become a brand spokesperson □ Save someone's life □ Rank the ways you wish to die □ Learn a sex trick from an animal □ Get a Green Card □ Sell your used knickers □ Change your name to Benrik by deed poll □ Go to prison today □ Work out your alcohol tolerance level □ Dance with death □ Write a love letter to your mailman □ Wear this "I'm lonely" sticker on your back □ Call a call centre in India for cultural information □ Get struck by lightning □ List all your friends and prune them □ Make a pact with the devil □ Communicate by ultrasound only □ Meet Anton □ Play Traffic Russian Roulette □ Give away free hugs □ Show and tell □ File a class action lawsuit □ Start your own religion □ Play corporate games □ Go above 100mph □ Eat something older than yourself □ Pass a note on public transport □ Sabotage Hollywood □ Add "von" to your surname □ Divine the will of your ancestors □ Make your boss notice you □ Make your heart beat faster □ Live by the Scout code of honour □ Make a non-obscene phone call □ Lobby Celine Dion to sing about you □ Join the French Foreign Legion □ Fine dine with Benrik □ Fabricate a prehistoric cave painting □ Attend court today and offer your verdict □ Found a new city □ Invent a new perversion □ Make the world a more beautiful place □ Get in touch with your hero □ Submit the stuff you'd like sent to Mars □ Defer to women in all things □ Predict the future □ Record something only you have noticed □ Practise zero tolerance □ Order off-menu □ Re-stage your birth □ Mutate to keep ahead of the pack □ Get mugged □ Let power corrupt you □ Ask public transport to make a detour for you □ Spy on your neighbours □ Solve a famous mathematical problem □ Call someone with a different phone area code and discuss your common bond □ Stalk someone □ Confuse a large corporation □ Work out how many seconds you have left to live □ Experience homelessness □ Arrive 3/4 of an hour late for everything □ Dress out of character □ Find a conspiracy in your everyday life □ Buy your own grain of sand in the Bahamas □ Enter the Nobel Peace Prize □ Invade people's personal space □ Think aloud all day □ Claim your own barcode □ Tell someone something they will never forget □ Find the Holy Grail □ Have a baby □ Recover your umbilical cord □ Investigate a news story yourself □ Trust strangers implicitly □ Breach the peace □ Make and test your own parachute □ Try to change fashion single-handedly □ Greet everyone as if they were a long-lost friend □

For detailed instructions, see the above

Life Planner

Plan your life from 0 to 77!* From your choice
of cot to your choice of coffin, there are a million
decisions to be made. Get your life in order here.

#	Crucial formative influences	#	First cigarette behind bike shed	#	
1		14		27	
2		15		28	Marriage and mortgage
3		16	Exams	29	
4		17		30	Party
5		18	Drink legally	31	Settle down
6		19		32	
7		20		33	
8		21		34	
9		22	End of youthful illusions	35	Itch (seven year-)
10		23		36	
11		24		37	
12	Puberty (girls)	25		38	
13	Puberty (boys)	26		39	

40	Party	53		66	
41		54		67	
42		55		68	
43		56		69	
44	Midlife crisis	57		70	Party
45	Take up golf	58		71	
46		59	Pay off mortgage	72	
47		60	Retirement party	73	
48		61		74	
49		62		75	
50	Party	63		76	
51		64		77	
52		65		...	

*Your average life expectancy

The history of the Diary

This Diary Will Change Your Life is now in its third modern edition, following a successful re-launch in 2004. As some readers might know, however, it has a long and distinguished history, full of drama, bloodshed and conspiracy. The essay below was researched by Dr Gunther Pedersen for Benrik Limited to mark the Diary's phoenix-like resurrection. We reprint it again here with the kind permission of his widow Clara, who herself unfortunately passed away in a ballooning accident.

The precise origins of THIS DIARY WILL CHANGE YOUR LIFE are a matter of academic dispute. So divided are scholars even as to its original title, the truth may never be conclusively established. Over the centuries it has been known variously as »The Book of Days«, »Fate's Very Own Calendar«, »Perish Ye Whom Glance Herein«, »365 Rollickin' Rides« and »Die Entdeckung der Weltgeschichte« – amongst many others. Nevertheless we will attempt to outline in broad terms its history, pointing out inconsistencies and gaps in our knowledge, bearing in mind along the way that, as the great Carlyle has said, ultimately »history is but a distillation of rumour«.

The first mention of the Diary is to be found in Herodotus, the Greek »father of history«, writing in about 450BC. He refers to »the curious custom practiced by the Pelasgians of following everyday of the calendar rites written on their oracle's tablets« (*Histories*, VI.56). Herodotus discusses the derivation of this custom: »I may say, for instance, that it was the daughters of Danaos who brought this ceremony from Egypt and instructed the Pelasgian women in it.« (II.171). The Pelasgians, of course, mentioned both by Herodotus and the more reliable Thucydides, are recognized as the majority tribe within the nomadic population of Greece and the Aegean, before their gradual assimilation by the Hellenes. There is therefore a strong case to suggest that the very origins of the Diary can be traced beyond the classical age and back to Egyptian civilization, the ultimate cradle of our culture.

Indeed, some have seen fit to speculate on the influence of the (as yet nameless) Diary on Egyptian history. Could Pharaoh Akhnaton's contempt for age-old tradition, for instance, stem from his worship of the Diary's ancestor? Certainly much has been made of the fact that when his sarcophagus was opened by the American amateur Egyptologist Theodore Davis in 1907, the unreadable remnants of twelve papyrus scrolls were found at his side. But there is no real evidence to back this claim.

At this point we should attempt to shed some light on two contentious issues. First of all, which of the multifarious versions is the genuine Diary? Fakes and translations are legion. For our purposes, the real Diary is the so-called Greek version, as found in Constantinople in 1422 by scholar Giovanni Aurispa (of whom more later). Both in depth and in originality, it stands out as the truest incarnation of the Diary, as anyone who cares to study it at the British Museum will surely agree (by appointment with the British Museum Special Finds Dept, London WC1B 3DG). We call it the »Original Diary«,

though no one has managed to pinpoint its ultimate authors (many have tried; see for instance H. Beckenbauer, »*The origins of the Diary: Atlantis revealed?*«, Eons Press, 1954).

Secondly, why is there so little mention of this ancient text in conventional histories? The answer will become readily apparent as we proceed; the Diary is essentially an instrument of radical change, unleashing forces too powerful for authorities to control. Thus it has been ignored and hidden away in official accounts; for those who look though, its footprints are everywhere.

Following Herodotus, the Diary resurfaces now and again in Greek fragments, essentially concerned with Orphism. Anaximander, for instance, tells us of γμγενειζ, »loosely translated as »The Book Of Days«. It is perhaps then no coincidence that Plato is the first to refer to it at any length, for we know he spent 12 years in Egypt and a deep understanding of Orphic cosmology permeates his works (his contemporary Krantor in fact accused him of lifting the *Republic's* political

hierarchy straight from the Egyptian caste system). In a little known appendix to his *Symposium*, he has prophetess Diotima of Mantinea argue the following: »What do you think, Socrates, of the study that Euthydemus and others make of that Phoebean text in which their pursuits are commanded day by day? Haven't you noticed how the course of their existence is varied, when so many people in Athens repeat everyday yesterday's actions again. Don't you agree?« »By Zeus I do!« said [Socrates]. »Well then, [said Diotima], can we say that this text is a medium for messages between mortals and the goddess Fate?« Socrates then goes off on something of a tangent regarding the parentage of said goddess Fate; but it is clear from this that the Diary was in use round about 400BC. It is also surely more than mere coincidence that it is mentioned in the course of the *Symposium*, famous for its emphasis on homosexual relations between males. Could some early Diary injunction to experiment sexually have caught on in Greek culture?

The Diary then enters a long period of obscurity, along with so many classical masterpieces. True, there is the odd reference to it in Roman texts; Cicero associates it uncritically with Epicureanism, accusing it of being »so easily grasped and so much to the taste of the unlearned« (*Tusculan Disputations*, IV, 3). But in truth it was more suited to the imaginative Greek spirit than to the more plodding organizationally-minded Roman outlook, and so never really caught on.

Of course throughout Antiquity the Diary was very much intertwined with religion. Early versions might have enjoined Phoenicians to sacrifice goats and suchlike. Indeed it is probable that the religious trend for issuing arbitrary instructions, such as the Ten Commandments, was derived from that very source. But it is with its rediscovery and adaptation in the Renaissance that it enters the modern age.

The Diary re-emerges – where else? – in Florence. Under Coluccio Salutati, Chancellor of Florence from 1375 to 1406, there came a new yearning for knowledge of the classical past. Few authors remained in circulation, with some quasi-extinct; there was only one known manuscript of Catullus in existence anywhere, for example.

In 1392, Coluccio himself found Cicero's »*Epistolae Familiares*«, which signalled the beginning of an intensive search for classical manuscripts. It was directed by Niccolo Niccoli, with the help of his right-hand man, the enterprising Poggio Bracciolini.

In the summer of 1416, Poggio visited St Gall, a 7th-century Benedictine monastery 20 miles from Constance in Switzerland. He asked to visit the library, which turned out to have been grossly neglected, »a most foul and dimly lighted dungeon at the very bottom of a tower«. As he leafed through the dusty old manuscripts, mostly in deplorable condition, Poggio's excitement grew. Here he had found a complete manuscript of Quintilian's *Training of an Orator*, substantial portions of Cicero, and a partial damaged Roman copy of something enigmatically named the »*codex diei*«, the book of days.

Poggio stayed at the monastery and copied it out himself with goose quills and inkhorn over 56 days. He then sent his copy back to Florence for which we must be grateful, as the original was lost in a monastery fire 7 years later. We are also in his debt for making it readable; the original, like most old parchment manuscripts, was copied out in minute Gothic text, which he exchanged for his own much rounder script (which

in due course became the basis of our modern handwriting).

It would be false to claim that the Florentines immediately recognized the value of the Diary, which is why it is hardly mentioned in contemporary accounts. This was partly because the Roman version they inherited was very much incomplete. Fragments such as »Today abandon all your pursuits in favour of the greatest good of them all ....chariot!« left them bemused rather than amazed. This all changed in 1423 when Giovanni Aurispa arrived in Italy with a vast hoard of original Greek manuscripts, 239 in all, including most of Greek literature: the *Iliad*, the *Odyssey*, Aeschylus, Sophocles, Euripides, Herodotus, Plato and countless others, all of a sudden given to Florence, along with of course the original Greek copy of the Diary...

This treasure chest of classical culture was seized, debated and lectured upon avidly by the Florentines. The young Greek scholar Marsilio Ficino translated Plato and the Diary, declaring the latter to be »one of the crowning achievements of classical civilization«. Indeed, his famous inscription in the hallway of the Academy, where the leading lights of Florence used to meet, was meant to bear witness to its influence: »Rejoice in the present«. Every citizen had a copy; Lorenzo de Medici had his bound in gold leaf. In retrospect, it is hard to resist the conclusion that the Diary contributed substantially to the conception of the individual that flowered in Quattrocento Florence. It enshrined the notion of »complete man«, one who realized all his innate qualities. It also chimed with the new Renaissance perception of time. The agricultural and monastical societies of the Middle Ages moved to the slow rhythm of the seasons and eternity. With their eye firmly fixed on the afterlife, they cared little for daily upheaval. But the Florentines were a manufacturing and trading people, to whom time was precious, to whom indeed time was money. It is no coincidence that a

Florentine, Brunelleschi, invented the alarm clock (in between painting masterpieces and building his famous dome). The Renaissance man lived for the here and now, and prized every moment. The Diary was part and parcel of this Weltanschauung.

Along with so much else in Florentine civilisation, the Diary met its nemesis in the form of Dominican friar Savonarola, who took Florence by storm in the 1490s with his apocalyptic preaching of hellfire and brimstone against the corrupt citizens who had abandoned the Gospels for more wordly pleasures and values. In Savonarola's vision of Florence as the new Jerusalem, there was no room for the impious free-thinking Diary. And in 1497, he tried to make sure all copies were burnt in his infamous Bonfire of the Vanities, along with copies of Boccaccio, Petrarch, paintings by Botticelli and other masterpieces. Almost all Diaries were thus consumed by the flames, and none would

likely have survived if he had held power much longer. But in 1498 he finally went too far and was excommunicated by the Pope, then hanged in the Piazza della Signoria and thrown on a bonfire of his own. The Florentine Renaissance was at an end.

Thankfully, one of the factors in its downfall also guaranteed its survival. When Charles VIII and the French Army invaded Italy in 1494, they were spellbound by the scale and beauty of the Florentine achievement: the Medici palace, the sculptors and painters, the tapestries... And so as conquering king, he shipped back to Amboise 21 craftsmen, manuscripts, pictures, over 34 tons of marbles – transplanting the Renaissance back to France.

The Diary went with him of course. It was in large part because the French held the original copy that Leonardo da Vinci accepted Francois I's offer to move to France from Italy in 1516, so that he could study it. For the next few centuries, the

under the absolutist reign of the Bourbon kings, the Diary held a much lower profile, and was considered mostly a quaint, even frivolous curio. Voltaire though saw its subversive potential and in 1778 translated it into French, none too scrupulously, adding much of his own trademark irony in the process.

CE JOURNAL VOUS CHANGERA LA VIE, as it had become, then re-emerged in the aftermath of the French Revolution in the unlikely hands of Donatien Alphonse Francois Marquis de Sade. Sade, of course, was an indefatigable scribbler himself and it will readily be perceived how the Journal's mix of arbitrary dictates fired up his imagination. A dozen days he wrote survive. The least unprintable enjoin followers to copulate variously with goats, toads, dwarves and grandmothers (the conceit here being to precipitate a fatal heart attack). Baudelaire claimed to have read the full-year Sadean version, describing it as a »veritable *Kamasutra* of pain«. No copy alas is extant.

The original Diary fell victim to Sade's notoriety and excesses. On March 6, 1801, Parisian police arrived suddenly to search the premises of Sade's publisher Nicolas Mosse, in hot pursuit of an obscure pamphlet, »*Zoloe*«, which Sade had allegedly penned against Napoleon and Josephine. The accusation turned out to be false, but the police nevertheless seized all the remaining stock of his novel *Juliette*, and of course his copy of the Diary. Napoleon, it seems, was ungrateful for this new acquisition, for he had Sade imprisoned without trial, and later transferred to Charenton insane asylum, where he stayed locked up until his death in 1814. In 1810, Napoleon punished him further by signing a decision to keep him in detention and forbidding all communication with the outside world, depriving him also of any writing materials. Whether this fate would have befallen him without the Diary is quite possible, but it is clear that Napoleon's unlawful confiscation of such a valuable manuscript helped consign the Marquis to political oblivion.

There is no record of Napoleon himself directly referring to the Diary, but there is no doubt he would have perused it; it is known that he liked books – even in difficult times at St Helena he had 3370 books in his library. But as Madame de Remusat informs us, he was »really ignorant, having read very little and always hastily«. The Diary's clear and concise orders would have suited his military temperament.

Few of his career-defining decisions can be traced directly to the Diary's dictates, with one exception: the Louisiana Purchase. Historians have always been somewhat puzzled by Napoleon's agreement to suddenly relinquish French possession of what was then called Louisiana but in fact encompassed 13 current states and over 900,000 square miles, for a relative pittance (15 million dollars). This was one of the greatest real estate deals in history, doubling the land size of the United States, transforming it into a world power and effectively ending France's dreams of worldwide presence overnight. No one was more surprised than Napoleon's finance minister, the Marquis de Barbe-Marbois, when he was instructed to reverse official policy on the morning of April 4, 1803. Perhaps if he had known that day's Original Diary entry, he would have been wiser: »Aujourd'hui, débarrassez vous d'une source d'ennui« (Today, try to get rid of something that bores you). Thus was the destiny of nations transformed in one stroke.

On a more general note, it is surely not coincidental that the year Napoleon acquired the Diary corresponds to that when his ego exploded: he was already First Consul by 1801, but by 1802 he had made himself Consul for Life, and by 1804 he was Emperor. Perhaps he took the Diary's emphasis on extreme individualism at face value. Some historians even posit he kept it close to his heart in his famous Imperial greatcoat, hence his famous position right hand tucked inside the tunic. Certainly, he took it with him on all his major campaigns, and indeed this is how it was acquired by its next owner, one Alexei Fedrovsky. As Napoleon retreated across the Berezina in December 1812 after his disastrous invasion of Russia, one of his staff officers, a Bordelais by the name of Ramballe, was hastily put in charge of the Emperor's remaining possessions as Bonaparte fled back to Paris in a fur-laden sleigh. Ramballe was immortalized by Tolstoy in *War and Peace*, where we find him ragged and near-delirious with his orderly Morel sharing a campfire with Russian soldiers near Krasnoe. Alas, he never made it back to Bordeaux. Like so many thousands, both French and Russian, worn out by the sub-zero temperatures and incessant gales, he froze to death drunk in the knee-deep snow on the roadside near Orsk, only ten miles from the Prussian border. The Diary was found amongst other papers by a band of pillaging cossacks, more interested in mens' boots than any obscure bundle of documents. They dumped the lot at their local billet, the castle of Alexei Fedrovsky, a count exiled from Moscow for political reasons in 1807. Alexei was famous for his imaginative cruelty: on at least one documented occasion, he sent his servants out early one morning to the local weekly village market, ordering them to buy up all the food available so that his peasant neighbours would have to starve for the week.

Fedrovsky was an early exponent of Russian political dissent, a radical before his time and more by temperament than ideology: he advocated the overthrow of Tsar Alexander on the grounds that his beard was not sufficiently manly. Rather like Sade, he was exiled at the insistence of his family, who kept finding their relative the laughing stock of Muscovite society. Nevertheless, Fedrovsky maintained links with the early precursors of Russian dissent. Though he did not make much use of the Diary himself (except when following its edicts could annoy his loved ones), he did pass it on upon his death in 1827, along with copious notes on facial hair throughout history, to his anarchist friend Bakunin. Bakunin was not yet quite the international firebrand and scourge of governments worldwide that he became in the 1850s. But he was still too impetuous and restless to sit down and take orders from a mere book. He was also permanently penniless, and thus it came that he gave the Diary away in exchange for some cabbage soup at the house of a friend of his in 1832. Fortunately, this friend was none other than literary critic Vissarion Grigorievich Belinsky, perhaps the man most deserving of the Diary anywhere on the planet at the time.

By the early 1830s, Russia was a moral and intellectual vacuum. The burgeoning young intelligentsia was desperate for spiritual nourishment, caught between the dumbly repressive autocracy of Nicolas I on the one hand, and the illiterate groaning peasant masses on the other. With no native role models to look up to, the Russian youth avidly absorbed every Western notion with a hint of revolutionary change. This was fertile ground for the Diary, and no one took it up more forcefully than their effective spokesman, Belinsky, the »conscience of the Russian intelligentsia« as Isaiah Berlin so aptly terms him. To Belinsky,

books and ideas represented salvation from the grim material philistine circumstances of Russian life. His was a philosophy of engagement; a man's life should reflect his beliefs, however much of a struggle was involved. Behaviour had to follow on from ideas. He lived in a state of permanent moral frenzy, of constant searching after the true ends of life. It is no surprise that the Diary, with its zeal for unending revolutionary experimentation and disregard for social conventions, appealed to him immediately. He copied out some of the more extreme days like »Go up to a member of the ruling classes and tell him how ignominious he is« or the religious-themed »God is dead. Make a small clay model of him and bury him in your back garden« and disseminated them amongst his friends and fellow radicals. He even penned a few pages of his own on the subject of serfdom (»Grab the nearest serf and run for the woods to free

him«, »Paint ›serfdom is the doom of the human spirit‹ on the wall of the Kremlin«). This sort of sentiment did not endear him to the Tsarist police as can readily be imagined.

And indeed it is reading out these pages of Belinsky's (and not merely his more famous 1847 »*Letter to Gogol*«) that got Dostoevsky condemned to death and sent to Siberia. By then, Belinsky had alas died of consumption. But such had been his influence that he can legitimately be called one of the founders of the movement that led to the Russian Revolution.

After his death, the Diary continued as one of the underground texts that fuelled the revolutionary fire across Russia and in the various places of exile where Russian radicals congregated. Though it has to be said that Belinsky probably best understood the essence of the Diary, which is its permanent encouragement of the flowering of the individual human spirit, the expression of the whole of man's nature, unfettered by the shackles of tradition. Later generations of revolutionaries were to put it to far more prosaic use, as we will see.

For the rest of the 19th-century, the Diary passed from radical to radical. It is difficult to know its exact history during this time as its successive owners were understandably publicity-shy and left few traces of their whereabouts and activities. The Populist-turned-Marxist leader Plekhanov seems to have recuperated it sometime in the 1880s. He in turn entrusted it to his star pupil Lenin, who found its radical tone of great comfort during his lonely years abroad in Geneva and Paris. Indeed it played a direct part in the Russian Revolution. During the 1905 uprising, Lenin had decided to stay abroad, obeying his more prudent instincts. When it came to the February 1917 uprising though, he consulted the Diary on February 12, which urged him thus: »Today plan a surprise trip somewhere hot«. Immediately, he resolved to set off for Moscow in the famous sealed train and changed the course of the Revolution, ending with the Bolshevik takeover in October 1917.

More generally, it is clear that the nature of Lenin's rule was influenced by the Diary, as reflected both in his ruthless drive and in the speed of his decisions. By the time Lenin died in 1924, he had grown mistrustful of both his comrades Trotsky and Stalin, and so bequested the Diary to Nicholas Bukharin, whom he called in his testament »the greatest and most valuable theoretician of the party«. His theorizing was no real match for Stalin's peasant cunning though, and the Diary soon got Bukharin into trouble. To be fair, it was no easy task to Sovietize what was essentially an individualistic bible, no matter how glorious its part in the history of the Revolution. Whole schools were given special versions, with tasks such as »Today, work to achieve the goals of the Five-Year-Plan« or »Dispose of ten kulaks by lunchtime!« (at the height of the collectivisation

hysteria in 1929). Yet this did not go far enough for Stalin. Unintentional lapses such as »How much do you love Comrade Stalin on a scale of 1 to 1000?« were seen as perilously close to inviting dissent, and undoubtedly contributed to the downfall and eventual execution of Bukharin. But there was worse to come for the Diary, or rather its bastardized Stalinist form. By the early 30s, such was Stalin's paranoia and fear of »Trotskyist contraband« that everything published (not just the Diary) was expected to be rewritten in his own personal style. Half the days in the 1934 »Correct edition« were about Stalin directly (»Compose a realist poem to the glory of the Revolution and its leader and nail it to an enemy of the working classes«). The other half were merely written in his plodding repetitious pseudo-scientific manner (»Today help organize your local communist associations with a view to undermining international capitalist superstructures«). Eventually fault was found with this edition too and its supervisor Sokolnikov was purged in the »Trial of the Seventeen« in 1937. Thus ended the sorry saga of the Soviet Diary.

Fortunately for us, the original emerged unscathed. Trotsky, who had seen which way the wind was blowing, managed to procure Bukharin's copy and took it with him in exile in 1929. He wandered for years, persecuted at a distance by Stalin who still feared his moral authority, until he eventually landed in Mexico. He found a house in Coyoacan near Mexico City with his wife Natalia Sedova. The Mexican Communist Party was strong but deeply divided into Stalinist and anti-Stalinist factions. Trotsky soon settled in, making friends with local sympathizers. He was particularly close to revolutionary muralist Diego Rivera and even closer to his painter wife Frida Kahlo. Rivera had helped Trotsky gain asylum in Mexico; they were comrades until 1938 when they split over ideological differences, and rumours of an affair between Trotsky and Kahlo.

Finally, history caught up with him when Spanish communist and Stalinist agent Ramon Mercador smashed his head with an alpine pickaxe on August 20, 1940, while he was writing an accusatory biography of his nemesis. Rather gruesomely, he did not die from the blow but stood straight up, screamed, and started pelting his assassin with everything within reach, including his dictaphone. His eventual death the next night went relatively unnoticed, as the world was understandably otherwise preoccupied at the time.

Trotsky's wife Natalia couldn't find the Diary after her husband's traumatic death. She suspected Stalin's agents had stolen it back, but the truth was closer to home. Frida Kahlo had indeed had an affair with Trotsky, in the course of which she'd borrowed the Diary. When the two of them broke up under suspicion from their spouses, she never returned it. Trotsky would not have been best pleased with her behaviour after his death: both her and Rivera showed little sympathy for him, seeking readmission to the Stalinist Mexican Communist Party and denouncing Trotskyism. Kahlo added insult to injury by slandering Trotsky as a thief and a coward. Her last painting was an unfinished portrait of Stalin, started after the dictator's death in 1953, and interrupted by Kahlo's suicide in 1954. By one of those minor quirks of which history is fond, the Diary then ended up in the hands of the FBI. Kahlo had died at the height of the McCarthyite hysteria in the US. Under heavy political pressure, all government security agencies were

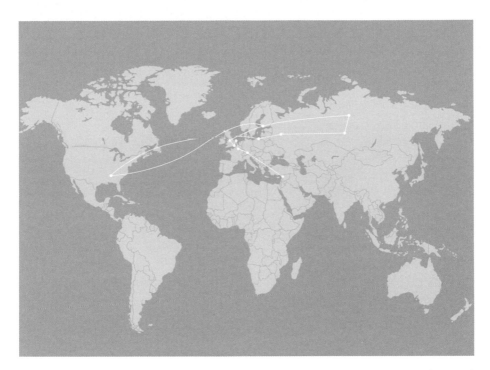

looking for reds under the American bed, particularly writers and artists whom everyone knew were susceptible to communist leanings at the best of times. Mexico was America's backyard. Naturally the spotlight fell on Rivera and Kahlo, artists of international renown with documented links to one of the chief instigators of the Russian Revolution.

J. Edgar Hoover himself, head of the bureau since 1924 and vehement anti-commie, took an interest in their activities, so that immediately upon Kahlo's death FBI agents in Mexico raided her house and made off with addresses of supposed Communist sympathizers, and Trotsky's copy of the Diary, no doubt regarding it as a timing masterplan for global insurrection.

The investigation into Kahlo's anti-American activities eventually petered out for want of firm evidence. No mention is made of the Diary, for the simple reason that Hoover kept it to himself. Like so many powerful men before him, he fell under its spell. Perhaps to those used to arbitrary authority and unquestioning obedience, submitting to the Diary's straightforward orders represented something of a liberation.

At any event, its influence on Hoover was more tragicomic than machiavellic. The entry that particularly caught his eye was March 24, 1958: »Experiment with forbidden fantasies«. The result saw him attending at least two gay orgies at the New York Plaza Hotel in 1958, wearing »a fluffy black dress with flounces and lace stockings and high heels and a black curly wig« according to one witness. He was introduced as »Mary«

and allegedly engaged in sex with boys as the Bible was read to him, throwing the Good Book down at climax. The latter claim is not considered reliable; but certainly the episode explains why the FBI had limited success against the Mafia during his tenure. With blackmail material such as this, underworld bosses Frank Costello and Meyer Lansky had little to fear from J. Edgar.

The Diary has lain in Hoover's classified files since his death in 1972. Under Exec. Order 11152, it was meant to be declassified 30 years later in May 2002. The FBI claim a clerical error prevented it from being found until November 2002, when it was finally made available to the public, and even then it languished at the bottom of a box in the FBI archive hall in Washington. It is only by amazing luck that the present authors, whilst engaged in a much larger authoritative study of the JFK Roswell cover-up, found it and decided to dust it off and update it for the benefit of the present generation. As with so much pertaining to this incredible artifact, it is impossible to tell whether the delay was deliberate.

One thing that history teaches us is certain: the Diary has always threatened various powerful groups by its very existence. May this new edition continue to do so.

Dr. Pedersen(1956–2003)

This Diary Will Change Everyone's Life!

Devotees of Benrik are encouraged to share the extreme self-improvement gospel with those hapless souls who have not yet discovered the Diary. Each Benrik reader must make it their mission to convert 3 others, who in turn will convert 3 more. Here you may record the Benrik tentacles as you help to spread them. Once you have filled in the whole chart, send it to Benrik, c/o PFD Literary Agency, Drury House, 34–43 Russell St, London WC2B 5HA, UK, and you will be invited to join the next stage of the Benrik cult.

BENRIK

Join the Benrik Cult

Many of the ideas in this Diary come from dedicated Benrik fans. Benrik's ultimate aim is to fill entire future editions with such ideas and retire to the South of France. If you wish to assist them, and see your name in minuscule print at the back of the 2007 Diary, visit the website and submit your idea for a life-changing task.

CONVERT

NAME...
SIGNATURE...................................

CONVERT

NAME...
SIGNATURE...................................

CONVERT

NAME...
SIGNATURE...................................

YOU

NAME...
SIGNATURE...................................

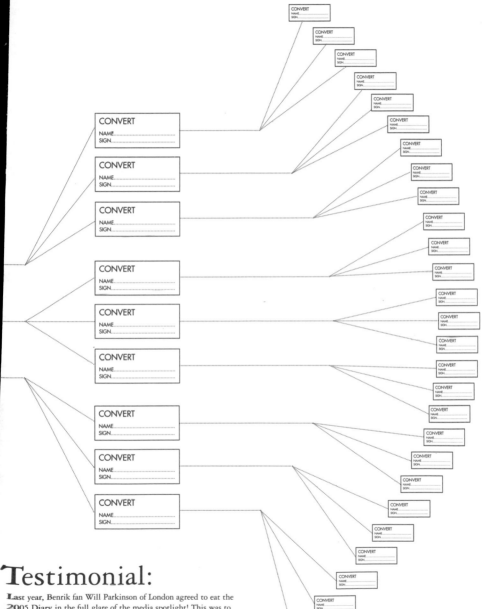

Testimonial:

Last year, Benrik fan Will Parkinson of London agreed to eat the 2005 Diary in the full glare of the media spotlight! This was to mark "Today, eat this book" day. It took Will a mere eight hours to munch through it, with the help of various condiments, and a blender. "I'd never eaten a book before, let alone for publicity purposes," stated Mr Parkinson. "My life has definitely changed."

All illustrations, photography, design and typography by Beurk, except as follows.